THE OTHER SIDE OF PARADISE

LIFE IN THE NEW CUBA

Julia Cooke

SEAL PRESS

THE OTHER SIDE OF PARADISE
Life in the New Cuba

Copyright © 2014 Julia Cooke

SEAL PRESS
A Member of the Perseus Books Group
1700 Fourth Street
Berkeley, California 94710

Library of Congress Cataloging-in-Publication Data

Cooke, Julia.
  The other side of paradise : life in the new Cuba / Julia Cooke.
    pages cm
  ISBN 978-1-58005-531-4 (paperback)
1. Havana (Cuba)—Social life and customs—21st century. 2. Havana (Cuba)—Social conditions—21st century. 3. Social change—Cuba—Havana—History—21st century. 4. Young adults—Cuba—Havana—Biography. 5. Havana (Cuba)—Biography. 6. Cuba—History—1990—Biography. 7. Cuba—Politics and government—1990- 8. Castro, Fidel, 1926—Influence. I. Title.
  F1799.H35C66 2014
  972.91'23—dc23

                    2013044413

9 8 7 6 5 4 3

Cover design by Raquel Van Nice
Interior design by Domini Dragoone
Printed in the United States of America
Distributed by Publishers Group West

To my family, y mi familia

CONTENTS

AUTHOR'S NOTE

Some names have been changed at the subjects' request, and in recognition of the reality of living in a one-party country. A few details of character and chronology have been changed, though not ones pertaining to real political people or specific news events. The facts remain true and nothing has been exaggerated or invented.

INTRODUCTION

There's a bar in downtown Havana, a backroom bar next to an outpost of the government-run Sylvain bakery chain where foreigners buy 65-cent bottles of water. The bakery used to sell flaky pastries, but a bite of their white frosting usually revealed toothache-inducing harshness, the sharp result of sugar and water hardened together without enough fat—bakers often lifted butter and oil to bring home on the occasions when these products arrived at Sylvain. And anyway, Cubans never bought pastries or water here—Cubans buy TuKolas and H. Upmann cigarettes, which the Sylvain still stocks, along with packaged chocolate and vanilla sandwich cookies and Nestlé ice cream. You could always find cheaper, better, flaky, and buttery pastries if you knew where to look, and now there are more small cafés and bakeries than ever in Havana, but TuKola is still so much tastier than peso sodas.

The bakery and the bar, El Caribeño, reside on the ground floor of a generic three-story apartment building whose corners are splotched with black mold. There are usually more people on the building's stairs than in the bar: when there's a flash rainstorm and people wait for fifteen minutes for the sky to clear, when no one has money for a drink or a TuKola, when apartments are hotter than streets. Russian Ladas are parked in the Partido Comunista de Cuba Parqueo next door. There used to be a small sign outside El Caribeño, palm trees curling parenthetically around the bar's name on the street corner, but it's been taken down. It was always easy to miss amid the much larger silver or neon signs for bars, restaurants, cabarets, music, music, music, attractions in this tourist-heavy neighborhood for visiting crowds of Canadians, Italians, Brits.

Here in Vedado, dark jazz clubs are lined in wood and velvet or mirrors. The ocean cups the *malecón* just down the hill from hotels where gangster Meyer Lansky hosted starlets and singers in the fifties, and white curtains billow around columns at restaurants in twenties sugar baron mansions. Vedado is casually suspended in the country's nostalgic past, shot through with *swing*, Cuban slang for charm, personality, style—even the slang reinforces the illusion! Sinatra could have sipped a daiquiri right over there, the palm fronds that crinkle in salty breezes seem to whisper. There are mansions with florid moldings and thick palm trees shading front yards, apartment buildings with porthole windows and delicate cantilevered stairs, broad balconies over which middle-aged women lean, squinting into the sun and smoking cigarettes that silk the street with Cuban tobacco. Some neighborhood structures have seen facelifts and paint jobs; others are scabby with patches of flaked-off paint that spread weekly.

The building that houses El Caribeño fits into the latter category. Water-toting tourists who poke their heads in usually don't enter. The Hotel Nacional's seafront patio with its rattan loungers, freshly cut lawn, and burbling fountain, with the wall of previous visitors like Naomi Campbell, is a block away. El Caribeño is open-air, too, but it's lit by fluorescent lightbulbs and furnished with sticky metal chairs instead of rattan and it's on a busy street across from the gutted high-rise Hotel Capri. A tang of metal hangs in the air from ongoing renovations at the Capri and the ocean is lost amid washed-out faces and scaffolding and persistent dust. The radio plays reggaeton or local pop, not the Buena Vista Social Club, and the only pictures on the wall are posters for local Cristal beer. But this place usually hosts at least a patron or two. Mojitos cost five pesos in the *moneda nacional* in which Cubans receive salaries, or 20 cents in Cuban convertible pesos, the Cuban tourist currency that's pegged to the U.S. dollar. Here, in a downtown area that caters to CUC-wielding tourists pleased with the price tags on $3 drinks, is a bar that locals can afford.

To be sure, they are not great mojitos. Bow-tied bartenders scoop four (five? six?) teaspoons of sugar into a glass with harsh peso rum, a squeeze of lime juice from a Tetra Pak box, an anemic stalk of mint, and a top-off of tap water. At least that's what composed my very first mojito, which I drank quickly at age twenty while pretending to understand my conversation with the two charismatic men who'd brought me and a friend to the bar and whispered the only phrase I did catch, that mojitos here were very cheap, just one dollar each. A long time later, I'd frequent a back table with a University of Havana alumna named Lucía and rotating clusters of students thrilled to pay someone to make them a drink. And a while after that, Adrián, a young jazz musician who lived across the street in an apartment owned by the (Che) Guevara family, would smirk when I suggested coming to El

Caribeño for a quick drink after one of our interviews. There were so many other, better spots opening since Raúl was in charge, he'd say. I would mostly walk past it, too, after I'd moved to Havana and started serving drinks at the apartment I rented, or stopped drinking mojitos altogether.

Havana reveals itself in snippets that build, one atop another, in a constant waterfall of places and scenes. Drink prices prove negotiable. The cluster of people outside a gas station or at a bus stop is an inflexible and enforced line. The Russian Lada or old American jalopy—a chugging Ford or Studebaker, with a mismatched door or hood ornament—is a taxi. That heavy stroller lugs not a husky baby but five dozen cups of black-market yogurt sold door-to-door from beneath a lace blanket. Consequently, the supermarket is the worst possible place to buy food, but gas stations are the most reliable spots to purchase cheap wine, except for the few months when the businessman helming the wine company dies under questionable circumstances and there's a diplomatic inquiry and production halts altogether and there is no cheap wine anywhere on the island. And this flexibility is ever more striking for its contrast with the essential fact of today's Cuba, the inescapable bearded face that's helmed the country for fifty-plus years, growing slightly grayer, jowls dropping yearly in portraits that get switched out and replaced but never taken down.

/// In 2006, Fidel Castro rounded the curve into his eighties and transferred presidential duties to his brother as he battled a vague but grave stomach illness and the dogged newspaper headlines that chased it: Intestinal bleeding! Stomach cancer! Surgeons stumped! Imminent death! The *Granma* state newspaper insisted that he would be fine, yet in February 2008, Fidel formally handed the reins to his younger brother Raúl and gave up the pretense of returning to office. Speculation fluttered, but few facts were known to the public other than that the new president had been the loyal and pragmatic minister of the armed forces for fifty years, and possessed not quite one-tenth of Fidel's charisma.

Raúl and Fidel and Che and the rest of *los barbudos*, the bearded revolutionaries, had pushed former president Fulgencio Batista and his coterie onto a plane—their wives still in New Year's Eve party dresses—a half-century earlier after the insurrection they'd begun when Fidel was twenty-six years old. Raúl had been twenty-two when they attacked the Moncada military barracks in 1953, the first violent strike against the old order, and Che had been twenty-five. Batista and the presidents before him, Ramon Grau San Martin and Carlos Prío, had billed themselves as revolutionaries, too, because Cuba's history as a constant colony lorded over by someone else was a convenient foil for someone who wanted to appear independent. But these new grizzly boys had both the age and the struggle to fit the title: They'd only ever lived in the Cuba that had failed to materialize after independence from Spain in 1899, the Cuba of extreme inequality and puppet presidents. They'd decided to fight. They suffered privations and violence to attain power, and their youth had amplified both their struggle and the changes they implemented when they won. What followed is common knowledge: socialism, expropriation of property or death to the ruling class, many of whom fled to the United States; reliance on the Soviet Union and strict regulation of citizens; an economic implosion when the U.S.S.R. crashed in 1991, and a slow accretion of change in the years since.

I started to learn Cuban history when I enrolled in a University of Havana class called "History of Cuban-U.S. Relations, 1901–1959." I'd taken a semester off from college to study in Havana, but, on my first day, I'd understood startlingly little of the rapid-fire Cuban Spanish as I sat at the front of a classroom of thoughtful twenty-year-olds who smoked cheap, unfiltered Criollo cigarettes from wrinkled paper packets in the hallways between classes. The chairs were made of dented metal and pressed plastic and bright sunlight flecked the floors with the imprints of the trees outside the open windows. The ceilings peeled, every student took assiduous notes on thin paper pads, and the only word I distinctly heard was *enmienda*, repeated over and over. So after class, I walked to a bookstore and found a middle-school history textbook. Later that night I flipped through page after page of illustrations and captions: "Workers were poor, illiterate, and miserable before the triumph of the revolution," "during the neocolonialist rule of the United States before 1959," "then cheering people greeted the guerrilla fighters," and "we love *Comandante* Fidel."

Enmienda, I learned, referred to the Platt Amendment, the 1901 American resolution to withdraw the remaining *yanqui* troops occupying Cuba after the Spanish-American War and establish the U.S. government's right to intervene in Cuban politics, turning it into a self-governing colony. But in that moment, the fluorescent lights—an initiative to replace all of the country's incandescent bulbs with energy-efficient Chinese models—hummed overhead, and I thought, *Every single young person that I will meet has read this textbook.*

Everyone my age sat under the same lightbulbs and had read the same book and I was hooked: Not only was Havana romantic and steeped in drama and history and humor, but it was inexplicable and strange and split from every cliché I'd heard or read about the city. Because the fact was, there was tremendous diversity, rebellion, and sophistication among the young people I met, both while studying at the University of

Havana and on visits and reporting trips in the years to come. Some danced salsa sinuously, though they couldn't afford to go to concerts at the Casa de la Música, the city's main tourist venue for salsa and casino. Others preferred to headbang in dilapidated amphitheaters on the outskirts of town among self-described anarchists. Nearly everyone wore jeans, not the threadbare Lycra shorts that news stories had cited. None of them drove old cars or could pay for rides in the glossy well-maintained Chevys that gleamed through the streets. They, and I, rode in 10-peso gypsy cabs or, more often, in packed buses on commutes that felt like being slurped up through a drinking straw, pushed toward the back by sheer momentum, and spat out only after hollering *"Chofe*, this is my stop!"* and elbowing toward the door.

Months after trust had built around study sessions and then drunken evenings and then political debates, I saw that the Cubans I knew passed around frayed copies of *People* or Spanish political rags, USBs loaded with Portishead or Daddy Yankee, carefully preserved copies of *The Unbearable Lightness of Being* between brown paper covers for discretion. I heard the complaints of a recent college graduate, my history instructor, Yoel, who for his lack of ideological zeal had been denied a job in international relations and was assigned to teach teenagers instead. His class held overt disapproval of U.S. neo-imperialist foreign policy and an oblique yet critical analysis of Cuba's one-party system. In the four years after I'd studied in Cuba, I moved to Mexico City, began to work as a journalist, and took a few reporting trips to Havana. When I searched for him on one such visit, he'd disappeared. The email address he'd given me bounced my letters back and no one at the university knew his whereabouts.

Brown paper cladding, discreet USBs, double entendre: the protective mechanisms of a well-adapted generation of

Havanans. Beneath the rambling discussions I had with young Cubans in bars and under weeping fig trees, on white sand beaches and at backdoor parties—the public places where Cubans were allowed to socialize with foreigners—history and politics thrummed, even in the mere detail of the fact that they, by law, were not allowed to enter my apartment, which was classified as a "hotel."

Absurdity was abundant: *Granma* came out every day with near-identical stories about Communist Party resolutions and policy revisions, and American newspapers published stories on "cyber-rebels" and independent libraries that no Cuban I knew had heard of, much less visited. The *Mesa Redonda* TV news program was on every night to decry whatever the United States had recently done in the Middle East, followed by old reruns of *CSI: Las Vegas* or *Gilmore Girls.*

I wanted to know what it was like to grow up in Havana in the last generation of Cubans raised under Fidel. I wondered how young adults felt when conformity was so encouraged, when kids at every school country-wide read identical textbooks and washed with the same soap and wore matching uniforms of white shirts with colored pants for boys and skirts for girls. All advertisements were controlled by a single political party. Every Havanan had at least one family member, whether distant or close, living abroad, but few young people had ever left the country—exit visas were not customarily granted to the under-eighteen set. And yet the isolation that defined their childhoods had begun to erode when they'd been adolescents: After the U.S.S.R. crumpled, leaving the country shockingly poor, the Cold War time capsule of Soviet-allied Cuba had opened to a tourism industry that filled hotels with Canadians, Italians, Brits, and Mexicans on tour packages. New treaties with China brought thousands for visits long and short. In 2008, Havana teemed with foreigners and change was already starting. Raúl legalized the sale of computers and cell phones to Cubans and began to tax the previously under-the-table payments that foreign companies had always made to local staff. Where it had been illegal for Cubans to enter hotels and tourist residences, Raúl struck down "tourism apartheid" a month into his presidency.

Havana was poised to shift away from what Fidel had shaped but forty-nine years in, its twenty-somethings had only ever lived in the city that failed to emerge from the promises of the Revolution. Not many wore beards—only *profundos*, the intellectual hippies, really had unkempt facial hair anymore—but the parallels were clear. I wanted to collect the stories of today's young Cubans in the fragile pillow of transitional time between Fidel and whatever would come next; I wanted a hint at what their Revolution could resemble.

/// Long after I'd discovered that you could buy five mojitos for a dollar at El Caribeño, not just one, I would spend a year traveling back and forth between Havana and Mexico City, conducting interviews that began just after Raúl stepped into the presidency. Reporting without the requisite government permits could get a foreigner trailed by the secret service and kicked out of the country, so I was as discreet as possible. Then, in 2009, I would move to Cuba with the help of a Party bureaucrat I privately called my Communist fairy godfather. I packed two suitcases and all the money I thought I'd need and I found an illegal apartment and learned where to buy groceries.

Havana captured my imagination because of its pervasive drama and uncertainty but also because of what I'd initially thought of as its layers. The bars I hadn't recognized as important, the informal mechanisms for traversing the city and procuring food, the people whose diversity and revolt emerged in well-hidden fragments—these details enticed and enthralled. Nothing in Cuba had clear associations with anything in my past. I never read anything that matched my experience of the place, freeing me to interpret alone, and time seemed to slow there, accordioning out in days and weeks during which my task was to edit those interpretations. No matter where I was during the years after my initial experiences in Cuba, some part of my mind remained in Havana. I could spend more time explaining how I now understand those initial reactions to Cuba as a product of my own upbringing and education in mainstream, upper- middle-class American society, or as a coming-of-age myself, a first bite of independence in a country so unlike my own—but that's not the point. The point is that long after the romance of being a stranger in a new land rubbed off, after gypsy cab price negotiations and black-market food purchases became frustrations indicative of larger ills, after I'd listened to so many stories of privations and indignities borne during the worst days of post-U.S.S.R. poverty and matter-of-fact recounting of families fractured across the Florida Straits, after I'd watched unexpected roadblocks smack down along carefully laid paths out of Cuba and even paths to better lives inside the country, after I began to suspect that I didn't know who surrounded me or what their intentions were, and after I started to yearn for something that simply was what it professed to be, without revision or footnote, grace remained. That grace was entirely created by the people in the following pages.

1

THE STORM

LUCÍA

Porosity is the inexhaustible law of life in this city, reappearing everywhere. A grain of Sunday is hidden in each weekday. And how much weekday there is in this Sunday!

—Walter Benjamin with Asja Lacis, "Naples"

Lucía was pretty pleased with herself. No real preparation, other than filling up a few two-liter plastic bottles with water now spiced with TuKola and lemon soda, and she'd slide through this *ciclón* just fine, she knew it. Well, she didn't know it, but she sensed that she'd get through Hurricane Ike the way she got through everything: clinging to the edge by fingernails, a big grin slopped across her face. Everyone else was scurrying and getting ready, hanging clothes, pegging boards to windows, waiting in line to clean out supermarkets that had held barely anything to begin with—what was the problem with not eating much for a few days? Her Brazilian medical student friends, twin sisters both named Ana, had gotten back into the country on one of the last flights from Mexico and would crash with her through the storm. They'd brought tortillas and, inexplicably, cans of tuna fish—inexplicable because this was one of the few things that Lucía and everyone else knew was reliably stocked at Cuban supermarkets—and Lucía had saltines and guava paste and her water. Now was when living on the very inside of a Soviet-style concrete block with windows that opened onto interior air shafts and other people's living rooms was an advantage, unlike every other moment she'd lived in this flat. Even if water licked inside the jalousie blinds that granted minimal privacy from the family in apartment 5D, even if her flat flooded, what would it damage, the fraying couch that wasn't hers? Her room had one tiny window and it was on the other side from where she kept her books. She moved her TV, pushed a few pieces of furniture away from the windows and closed up as tight as she could; otherwise, she sat and read a bit and talked to the Anas and waited.

Four tropical storms had pushed through the Caribbean in August alone. Now it was a September Monday in 2008 and Hurricane Ike blustered straight at Havana. Not straight at the city, to be fair, but it had touched down that morning on the northeast coast of Cuba as a muscular category 4 storm and no one was sure where it would head from there. It was expected to tear up the east, continue southwest, and barely avoid Havana and the two million inhabitants in and around the city. Or it could swerve in and hit the city itself, an unpredicted tantrum but possible.

I'd arrived a few days before and though I'd met Lucía years earlier at University of Havana parties, I wouldn't see her until just after the storm. From where I sat on the porch of the ground-floor Vedado apartment where I rented a room, the street shuddered from the crisp dry waves of heat. The clouds and humidity were gone, as if the storm had slurped up every drop of moisture. Cubans scrambled through the streets; the small clusters of prattling neighbors or school-mates that usually hovered on corners, benches, retaining walls, under boughs of bougainvillea, and on steps, enacting Havana's characteristic languor, had never assembled that morning. People waved instead—curt arm gestures, a nod of the head—or hollered a shrill word or two as they passed.

Throughout Vedado, rangy shirtless men climbed lad-ders to hammer sheets of plywood against floor-to-ceiling panes of glass. Laundry lines sagged from upstairs win-dows. Worn T-shirts and heavy jeans flopped in the wind—housewives had done their washing and mopping in anticipa-tion of the days to come, when they wouldn't have water for cleaning or sun for drying. The clacking sound of dominos hitting card tables had disappeared along with the hoots of the men who played everyday games on the strip of dirt and hardy grass between the sidewalk and street; they'd noted scores and would resume in a few days. One newscaster's insistent monotone floated through open doors and windows. On TV, he shooed a gray triangle across a map of Cuba to demonstrate the likely path of destruction. Ike would just skim Havana.

The tall *señora* of my *casa particular* smelled like perfumed soap and competence as I approached her in the kitchen. Her two preteen sons mostly stayed in the bedroom that her mother-in-law would share with her, her husband, and their two children while I inhabited their second bedroom for $30 per night. I watched as she peeled potatoes, asking what I should do to prepare for the storm. Stockpile water? Buy canned food? Cubans knew hurricanes, she said—"Nothing, *m'ija*, nothing at all." Of course she'd be taking care of me, she smiled as I hovered awkwardly. She'd boiled water for me to drink. Remember how she'd written down my passport number in that logbook for the authorities? She was accountable while I was in Cuba, she said before turning away. I wasn't to worry; she'd keep me safe. So I left the house.

This Havana was sharply active, confident. As Hurricane Ike rapped at the door, promising to push a few of the city's old buildings to their knees, scenes seemed to have postcard-crisp edges. A dozen people outside every gas-station convenience store enacted the *último* system, the way that Cubans form lines outside stores and bus stops: The last person to arrive and join the milling group shouts *último*; whoever was previously last in line raises a silent hand; and the new last person takes his or her place as the *último*, to be unseated by the next to arrive.

But by late afternoon, people had disappeared, pulled dry clothes inside, and shuttered windows. Whiteboards outside the Coppelia ice cream parlor announced flavors—*Almendrado, Avellana, y Vainilla*—to phantom crowds. The only sound was the wind, rattling loose beer cans down the street and shaking the leaves of trees like an eerie symphony of hundreds of newspapers crumpling in unison. In the ocean, frothy whitecaps nicked the water's surface.

Electricity and water had been shut off throughout the city that afternoon. Back at my *casa*, my *señora* had filled a tank, stocked candles for every room, and left a pitcher beside my bed. She moved assertively, cooking and entertaining her children and elderly mother-in-law in the dark. The old woman's home had been deemed unsafe to ride out the storm by the local Committee in Defense of the Revolution (CDR), the neighborhood pipeline from street to government, of which there was one office per block.

When I peered out of my room a few hours later, my *señora* sat in her nightgown in a rocking chair at the end of the hallway. The ten-year-old perched in her lap, his legs splayed out to the sides of hers. He held a book close to his pert nose in the yellowish light. Outside, I had never seen Havana's nighttime streets so empty, as if waiting for a shootout. A tinny clanging sound, something loose on the neighbor's roof, announced the storm's arrival.

/// Lucía and seven of her friends sat in the living room of her sixth-floor flat, sipping one weak, warm rum and cola after another, smoking cigarettes, and laughing while the rest of Havana played out the human dramas born of too much family time. Their only source of news on the storm was what they overheard through the open windows of the apartments around them. Hours had lost shape and meaning once the eye of the storm had passed through about fifty miles from Havana on Tuesday morning and left only minor damage in the city. What began on Tuesday afternoon as two friends walking over to Lucía's to hang out with her and the Anas had become on Wednesday a slightly tipsy band of parlor-game-playing refugees from their jammed family apartments, nagging mothers and aunts and exiled elderly relatives who didn't seem to mind being stuck at home, dads and uncles who sat on front couches and drained bottles of peso rum.

Electricity and water wouldn't return to Havana for a few days, though only sixteen buildings were downed city-wide. In those that had solidly withstood the storm, the hurricane parties were in full swing. Among young adults in Havana, where you spend a hurricane is an issue that's more about socializing than safety.

Chaos consumed the countryside to the east. More than two and a half million Cubans across the island had left their homes, decamped on orders to find somewhere safer. Nearly ten thousand tourists had repacked rolling suitcases and moved from hotels in the storm's path to other government-owned resorts. Hurricane Ike had destroyed thousands of houses; pulled up harvests of rice, beans, plantains, and sweet potatoes; shattered half a million eggs and killed a million chickens. Cuba reported its first storm-related human fatalities in years: four people dead in the provinces. The count was in the high double digits in Haiti. Later, the cost of the storm's damage to the Cuban economy would be estimated at $7.3 billion.

This was some of what I told Lucía on Wednesday afternoon when I knocked on her door around noon. Boredom and impatience had sent me deep into my address book and Lucía, a friend of a friend, was the only person I knew who was home. She hadn't left her apartment since Monday.

"Is water on anywhere?" she asked as I walked in.

"Next word: *Triscaidecafílico,*" a voice called out from the kitchen.

"Water but no electric," I said.

"I won't get water until we get electricity," Lucía said, as if gesturing toward an apology for what her nose now failed to detect as her own body odor. One of the people in the room pushed a drink into my hand. They were three statuesque ballerinas, the Brazilians, the boyfriend of one of the women, and Lucía, who wouldn't have been mistaken for a dancer: medium height, slightly pudgy, but pretty, with intense light-brown eyes beneath high, naturally defined eyebrows, pale skin salted with freckles, and a crooked, sudden smile.

"Oye, triscaidecafílico!" the voice hollered and everyone quieted down and began to scribble on the sheets of paper they held.

"A midget who lives on the third floor of . . ." said one ballerina a few minutes later.

"An orgasm induced by a three-fingered man or woman," and on and on, each of them offering up a faux definition in a homemade version of Balderdash.

Lucía lived alone in an apartment that wasn't hers. The flat was a light-deprived space furnished with two torn plastic couches under molding ceilings and a bucket in lieu of a shower head. Ash streaks clawed up her kitchen walls from the time she'd blown up a pot making rice while drunk, but it was a place no one else called home.

After graduating the year before from the University of Havana, Lucía was putting in the two years of social service that "paid for" the degree. She should have been sent back to Ciego de Ávila—the town where she'd grown up, right around the knuckle of the crooked finger of Cuba—to live at home, as all unmarried young people did. The only way to get an apartment of your own was to register on the never-ending list for state-granted homes and wait: years, decades, possibly never if rules were followed in overcrowded Havana. The government kicked most people from the provinces who didn't have permits to live in the capital right back to the country. But she'd asked a friend's mother if she could list their house as her official address in Havana and the papers had gone through the system unnoticed. Then she found an apartment that family friends from Ciego wanted to rent so they could retire back home with a steady income. They shared a last name and so when inspectors came around, she claimed to be a cousin.

She paid around $100 per month, which she earned by renting out her spare room via word of mouth and an Internet forum for shoestring travelers. Foreign backpackers and freelance photographers relished having a *Cuban experience* at a rate of $10 a night. These were all punishable offenses, but Lucía had a way of making people want to do things for her, with her. Her friend's mom had begun to claim the Havana-residence-registration plot as her own idea.

If Lucía had been born in a different place, or in the Cuba that didn't exist but might have had certain twists and turns of history gone differently, her career trajectory could have, hypothetically, gone like this: She'd have moved to Havana, waited tables or tended bar while working toward her degree, and wound up managing the restaurant or bar. She'd have quietly done favors for people whose quid pro quo mattered and would find herself in her early thirties a well-paid producer or manager of some sort, possibly mid-level in an entertainment empire or maybe at hotels or a media conglomerate.

But that Cuba certainly wouldn't exist at least until Fidel died, and who knew if it could come into being even afterward? Lucía wasn't waiting to see. She was twenty-five. Her twenties would be over before she blinked and the old man could hold on until well into her thirties. She didn't want to still be "inflating balloons," as she called what she did every day at the Cuban national TV station: preparing managerial reports, manipulating data at the behest of higher-ups to reflect a brighter outlook than reality. Her salary was $12 per month, deposited directly into her Banco Central de Cuba account, but she also got a desk with an Internet connection. So she arrived around noon on weekdays, left by four, and hushed up in between, because she had a plan, and she couldn't act on that plan until after she successfully finished her social service.

The smell of cigarettes, sweat, and spilled TuKola, Cuba's sugary riff on Coke, fermented in Lucía's apartment and someone suggested heading out to the *malecón*. A few clusters of people already dotted the curve a block or so apart. Once cash had been collected for another bottle of rum and the ballerina and boyfriend had gone off to find an open store, the Brazilians began to talk about their hometown, Recife, where they'd lived until moving to Cuba for scholarships at the Latin American Medical School. Lucía had met Ana Two on a bus heading back to Havana from Ciego, when the line had been too long and she'd asked the youngest person in it if she could cut with them. Ana had said yes.

Ana One, who wore her hair in braids, swept her arms across the horizon as she told us that their city was built right on a beach, rather than a seawall. People walk around in bikinis, added Ana Two, whose hair was brushed out and pulled into a ponytail. Which made the group pause to reflect: What if Havana had been built on the other side of the port, the one closer to the eastern beaches? What if Havana were graced with sand instead of this, its *malecón* promenade, the city's collective couch and the rocky shore below?

"There would have never been a Revolution," said Lucía, with a clap of her hands. "*Imagínate*, with all of that tourism, with that kind of economy and setup, Fidel and Che and Raúl never would have gotten anywhere." Everyone laughed, murmured in assent, and then paused awkwardly, the pillow of empty time that hovered around politically sensitive statements made in large groups with newcomers. Imagined scenes of a Havana that resembled a Spanish colonial Ipanema unfurled into the silence.

Lucía poked the air with her index finger. "And the point is, obviously, *caballero*, obviously, that it's thanks to the *malecón* that we have the triumph of the Revolution!"

/// In the days following the hurricane, the U.S. government pledged battered Haiti $10 million in aid. Cuba was offered $100,000 and a promise of more if the country allowed a U.S. team in to assess the damage. President Raúl Castro, who'd worn his new title for only six months, said no. All Cuba needed, he said, was for the restrictions of the fifty-year-old trade embargo to be provisionally lifted so the country could buy food and building materials on credit. While it was legal to buy certain items (medicine, food, construction goods) from U.S. businesses through a humanitarian loophole, they had to be paid for in cash. Under the embargo, companies from third-party countries that traded freely with Cuba could be subjected to fines and their executives denied visas to travel to the United States.

Washington's response was no. The embargo wouldn't change unless human rights improved and political dissidents and anti-Castro journalists were released from jail. Throughout the week, newspapers across the United States, except in southern Florida, published editorials and op-eds: The foolishness of a policy that hadn't achieved its goal of regime change in Cuba in half a century seemed magnified in Ike's wake. The appearance of such articles alongside news of booming imports from China, Cuba's new political ally and role model, highlighted the political insincerity being criticized. But the fact that public discussion of an outdated American policy toward Cuba did not spark retribution from the more militant Castro critics in the U.S. spoke of a shift in the swirl around the politics, a distinct cleft between the then and the now. *Then* was a time, thirty years ago, when pro-engagement editorials in *El Diario–La Prensa* resulted in exile-made bombs exploding at the paper's offices on New York City's Hudson Street. Then was when an American citizen, a Cuban American who lived in Union City, New Jersey, could be killed with semiautomatic artillery in front of his thirteen-year-old son on a suburban street—the mind conjures images of a cul-de-sac, a picket fence sloshed with red—for participating in dialogue with the Cuban government. In the now, these editorials inspire scoffing and angry discussion. In the now, former Hialeah mayor Raúl Martinez, running that fall for a Miami-area seat in the House of Representatives, urged the Bush administration to relax restrictions on remittances and travel in response to Ike's devastation.

The embargo stood solid and unchanged, less an effective public policy than a legal expression of a collective wish. In November, Martinez lost the election with 42 percent of the vote. Throughout Cuba, "The Revolution is more powerful than mother nature!" appeared in a cartoonish font, scrawled brightly across walls in the weeks following Ike.

Lucía had heard the language of this political drama for as long as she could remember words, seen cartoon images as a child not of Charlie Brown but of Uncle Sam being admonished for his neocolonialist ways, played along as emergencies ranging from imminent invasions from the North to hurricanes either happened or dissipated into little but expended energy. That Thursday night, two days after the hurricane, she and her friends were less interested in Washington than in jumping the line to get into the Turf Club. Bus service had just begun and little was open after the storm. All the lights on the walk between my *casa* and Turf were out. But beneath the glimmer of the three functioning streetlights on the dark block, around forty people swarmed into a disorganized queue. A fuzz of conversation arched above the crowd, which funneled toward a bouncer at the stairs above the doors of a basement club, which burped out intermittent bass chords when anyone entered or left.

Within moments of arrival, I was pushed up against the sticky chain that barred the entrance—Lucía had hollered above the din and pulled me through the crowd to join her group at the front. She passed me a tepid green plastic bottle filled with rum and lemon soda and waved a greeting to someone who'd joined the line behind me. Water was back in most homes. Those who hadn't showered had applied abundant perfume.

Turf was dilapidated, maze-like, and so thoroughly soaked in cigarette smoke that the walls reeked. But on Thursday nights, when a DJ spun Justin Timberlake, Lynyrd Skynyrd, local rappers Los Aldeanos, and on and on, it attracted pop musicians, children of the government elite, Lucía and her foreign friends, university students, artists—*los miki*. Mainstream, cool-hunting Havanans. Lucía spent money on the $3 cover fee for Turf rather than a package of toilet paper for home—they cost about the same amount and *Granma* was printed on thin soft stock.

Past the bouncer, a bow-tied, waistcoated man stood at an old-fashioned cash register taking the cover charge. The dance floor beyond was lit by two mandarin-toned lamps set into the low ceiling and a flashing light that thrust the room into intermittent half-darkness. People shimmied and sang along to the English lyrics of Amy Winehouse: "Rrrrehab, I said! No, no, no." Girls' tank top straps slipped from their shoulders and boys mopped their foreheads with shirt hems. Nearly everyone wore Converse or Adidas tennis shoes.

It was hot enough that night that when my arm brushed anyone else's, we traded a film of sweat. The ceiling peeled, uneven patches of solid blue slipping away to reveal an archaeology of paint jobs. Brown, red, and farther down, the grainy white concrete of the structure itself. The seating area just past the bar that separated the dance floor from the tables, where I sat with a group of Lucía's friends, was stifling.

"You know what they call Raúl Castro," Mari said to me, leaning in to the table. Mariselys, with a perky voice and shiny hair, was a lawyer but hadn't practiced since finishing her social service the year before. She managed a pop band and would soon marry a Frenchman. She wanted Lucía to take over the band—"she'd be perfect at it, wouldn't she?"— but Lucía, Mari said, was planning to leave Cuba around the same time as she. "Raúl is Julio Iglesias," she continued. "Because *la vida sigue igual*"—(life stays the same, the title of a collection of his first hits).

"The only thing that changes here is who's sleeping with whom," said Lucía. Whether this was due to Raúl Castro or the U.S. *bloqueo* didn't matter. Neither side could be trusted. What one saw, heard, did, felt, or needed held weight, not what *Granma* said, not what Washington said.

A little before 2 AM, the DJ interrupted a Beastie Boys song to instruct everyone to leave the club. A collective groan floated up and Lucía's friends looked around. People began to shuffle out. This was unusual, ridiculous, they muttered. Turf stayed open until at least three, sometimes later. Lucía, Mari, and I waited outside, collecting her friends one by one until we all crowded together, one node of the multitude that stood in the empty street. Lucía turned around in a circle, trying to find out what had happened. A neighbor had complained, someone reported. The block's CDR had dispatched an official to chastise the club management. Since the rest of the neighborhood still didn't have power, it looked overly decadent to allow the cover charge–paying youth to keep dancing. Three dollars was almost a week's pay on a government salary.

Whether or not that was the real story was irrelevant. Getting information in Havana was a game of telephone in which a snippet of news from a well-connected acquaintance, read on a foreign news website or seen on CNN in a hotel lobby, was circulated via word of mouth. News that came from the collective weighing, editing, and fact checking of the rumor at hand would always be more valuable than what the government called "truth."

The crowd of about a hundred partiers dispersed into the night unfazed. Lucía and Mari hitched rides to a friend of a friend's house, the Nuevo Vedado home of a well-known artist whom someone was sleeping with, where Brazilian modernist chairs sat beneath paintings that sold in blue-chip Manhattan galleries. The rest headed to the *malecón*, to the nearby University of Havana dorms, to any place but home.

/// Not everyone in Havana had access to dollars, which were necessary to buy toilet paper or go to Turf. The use of U.S. currency was a relatively new phenomenon: Though dollars had existed in Cuba before the nineties, sent by family members who lived abroad and stashed inside mattresses or behind loose bricks, it was illegal to use or even own *yanqui* money until a few years after the fall of the U.S.S.R. The Revolution had distanced itself from the only paper currency that had been in general circulation on the island until 1934—the peso had been introduced in 1914 but wasn't widely used until after the Great Depression.

Prior to the nineties, Soviet subsidies had held the Cuban economy aloft while a certain sense of idealism dominated the national consciousness. Literacy rates hit 99 percent and for the first time in history, all Cuban citizens had health care. The ration booklet provided over a hundred monthly necessities and there was little crime. Cuba was also a police state whose one political party had a rigid grip on nearly everything. Plenty of people opted out even back then, but, while Havana before 1990 was by no means perfect, older Cubans have told me in rose-tinted lament, at least there was a sense of upward trajectory.

When the U.S.S.R. dissolved in 1991, Cuba lost around 80 percent of imports and exports and over a third of its gross domestic product. The government dubbed this economic crisis the "Special Period in a Time of Peace" and tried to cope. Its main tactic was to embrace foreign currency and coax tourists back to the island. In 1993, the government legalized the use of the U.S. dollar. When it did, the egalitarian society that Fidel Castro had tried to create was cleft by a distinct, unarguable economic disparity; haves and have-nots depending on one's access to dollars and anyone who had them. Lucía had been ten years old then, and her memories were hazy. Electricity was cut because the government couldn't afford more than a few hours each night and summers were so hot without fans that her family dragged their mattresses to the sidewalk in hopes of catching nighttime breezes. After dinner one night— she had cooked, and I had given her $5 to buy the black-market lobster tails that we ate atop pasta with pepper and scoopfuls of butter—she told the Canadian in residence and me about an uncle who'd taught her to churn butter from the black-market milk he brought over. The Special Period didn't hit as hard in the countryside as the city, and Lucía had an aunt in Venezuela who sent what dollars she could spare. Lucía was a have, though she hung there by the barest of threads.

Implausibly, Cubans got by, even if adults lost an average of 5–25 percent of total body weight between 1990 and 1995, as a Canadian study found, even if they marinated, fried, and ate banana peel "cutlets" for dinner, even if thirty thousand rafters took to the seas in rickety, dissipating skiffs in 1994 alone. By September 2008, there were two Cuban currencies. Dollars had been dispensed with as the government cited the need to retaliate against further sanctions from Washington, and the Banco Central de Cuba printed the CUC, which Lucía and everyone else called *kooks*, *fulas*, or *chavitos*. The rainbow-hued *kooks* were printed on thick stock and embellished with holograms. They were worthless outside Cuba, since they weren't recognized by any international bank.

One CUC bought 24 pesos in *moneda nacional*: flimsy slips of paper in which local salaries were doled out and basic goods like sugar and rice and vegetables grown in Cuba were sold. The green, 1-peso bills were always rumpled and sweat-stained; the red, hundreds were often crisp, unsullied by frequent use. Average monthly salaries in Cuba hovered around 300–400 pesos per month, or 12–16 *kooks*. Although foreigners rarely used *moneda nacional*, Cubans had to use *kooks* if they wanted imported goods. Shampoos and deodorants, packaged foods, chocolate, toilet paper, most cleaning products, and milk—the government provided milk rations only for children under seven years old—were all sold in *la chopin*, the CUC stores, where everyone went shopping.

The Special Period had taught Cubans to *resolver*. In the gulf between literal and colloquial meanings, to *resolver* implies questionably legal activities, since at least one step of nearly every solution to any problem in Havana today involves the black market, and always indicates an exchange of favors. Sentences in Havana would feel barren without *resolver*, for example, "I can *resolver* that for you" or "¿Resolviste?" meaning "Did you get ———— sorted out?" You could *resolver* in order to seek pleasure and fun or to acquire more prosaic necessities. It could be a mutual activity, too. When I left my *casa particular* for a cheaper one in dusty Centro Habana a few days after Hurricane Ike, my *señora* didn't charge me for my meals—a different permit was required to serve meals to foreigners and she'd have to show the government her receipt logbook. She just told me to chip in what I thought was fair. *Me resolvió; le resolví.*

/// Lucía's office soon cut off Internet access for all but its highest-level employees, she told me one afternoon in the lobby of her pistachio-colored office building next to the artisan street fair where vendors sold toy cars made of beer cans and ashtrays with Cohiba cigar logos. She shuffled her feet in her plastic flip-flops. The distance between her shoulders and her toes seemed shorter than usual. She avoided my gaze and stood in awkward silence, and when finally I said I was hungry and wanted to grab some *croquetas* at Pollo Ditú next door and did she want to come along, she shook her head, gave me a small, bleary smile, and said she had a little more work to do and we parted. Walking away, she looked like a dog who'd lost its owner and run out of energy circling the park to look for him. Lucía needed the Internet to implement her plan to leave Cuba.

She needed to be in touch with some family friends in Chile, who had offered to write her the *carta de invitación* that she'd need to travel abroad. Once she finished her social service, she could apply for her *tarjeta blanca*, her exit permit, and if she could pay for a visa and a plane ticket and a little bit of money to start off, she could leave. Lucía's thirties would, she hoped, find her settled into whichever country offered her a visa first: Chile or maybe Spain. New legislation offered Spanish passports to the grandchildren of political exiles who'd left under Franco's rule; one of her grandfathers had settled in Cuba from Spain. She had a year of service left.

Within a week or so, she'd send a text message to the cell phone I rented from an entrepreneur who rented her family's phones to short-term foreigners. Lucía's own cell phone, a gift from a tourist who was due for an upgrade back home, unlocked from its home network by a computer programming student in a fourth-floor Old Havana back room, was rarely charged with enough prepaid funds to send messages, so her texts often came from anonymous numbers. "Concert at Bertolt Brecht tonight 9 PM outside come this is Lucía." She'd gone home that one sad afternoon to lie in bed and read one of the many books that she stacked on stolen milk crates next to her twin bed. Then she'd watched *Friends* and a pirated Kusturica film on her tiny television. She'd left the cleaning until the following day, and then the next, because she had no foreigners staying and couldn't get any more until she could check her email—an hour on a hotel computer cost $8 that she didn't have.

Then a friend came over. Someone always came over. Sometimes it was her upstairs neighbor Claudio, who could talk his way into or out of absolutely any situation in Havana, who'd come downstairs to lie on her couch to read, too, because he lived with a grandmother whose presence sometimes became oppressive. Then Lucía would eventually come out and sit there being miserable and hopeless with someone else—Claudio had dropped out of school at age fifteen and therefore couldn't work or leave or do anything else but talk or read, really, both of which he did voraciously, single-mindedly, rapidly. Then she'd be convinced to go with him to whatever was happening in Havana at night. As long as there was something going on somewhere, a 5-peso concert at Bertolt Brecht, a free open mic night out in Miramar, a drag show at Parque Lenin, any spectacle at all, she was fine. She'd use a single spritz of Estée Lauder Sunflowers, of which her aunt sent her free-gift samples, pull her hair in a ponytail, and go, and, eventually, after a few days, she'd feel better. Eventually, Lucía would *resolver* the Internet situation.

The Anas registered for an in-home Internet access code, which was limited to foreigners; a Cuban filmmaker friend of Lucía's offered to split the bill if he could use half of their monthly allotted hours. Lucía spent a little less time at her office, now. The connection was slow and the line was usually busy so she often spent afternoons at her friend's place in an attempt to connect.

Young Havanans weren't waiting for Julio Iglesias. They were *resolviendo* their way through hurricanes and sometimes even from small towns in the middle of the country to Spain or Chile.

2

UNDER THE TABLE

CARLOS

"I think I know who can find you an apartment," Lucía said.

I sat on her couch picking at fraying white vinyl. My address book lay open on my knees. I'd moved with a ten-month student visa, plans to take a weekly class on popular culture, two suitcases and visions of a terrace, and balustrades, an apartment close to a main bus and *máquina* line, preferably in Vedado. After two weeks I'd found nowhere to live. A legal resident foreigner could rent only from an authorized *casa particular* owner or directly from the state, apartments priced for businesspeople and reporters on expat packages and usually bugged. A "real estate agent" with frosted pink lipstick set foreigners up in long-term *casas* and took a cut; she shook her head when I told her I hoped to pay less than $25 a night for a monthly rent. On a full apartment! She didn't return my calls. Foreign students lived in crowded *becas*, dorms, but anyone who could afford to stay elsewhere did—the Anas had moved into an apartment of their own and I was by now too old for dorms. Lucía was my Yellow Pages, my best hope to map out opportunities.

That weekend the government tossed the city into a forty-eight-hour "national time of mourning" after *Comandante* Juan Almeida Bosque's fatal heart attack a few days earlier. Concerts and parties in all state-owned venues were cancelled for the forty-eight hours following the death of the eighty-two-year-old: third-ranking government official, guerrilla commander from the 1959 Revolution, highest-ranking Afro-Cuban in government, lover of literature and music. He'd composed upward of three hundred songs himself. Maybe this justified the fact that hotel cabarets and bars catering to tourists stayed open. But locals were supposed to mourn. That afternoon, as the middle-aged driver of my *máquina*, collective taxi, had circled the *plaza de la revolución*, where thousands of older Cubans had queued up to pay their respects, he broke into an Almeida-written song in a voice quavery as an old record. "Sure, he was just another old man revolutionary," he'd said slowly when he finished the verse. The other Cubans in the back seat had offered a few claps. "But Almeida was special."

"Super fula," crazy fucked up, was Lucía's take. But since everyone would be on G Street that night, she could introduce me to Carlos, whose mother rented out a small apartment.

The avenue's broad, grassy median, where every weekend young people gathered to drink and gossip, was so full with teenagers and young adults that night that people walked in the gutters, shuffling through discarded cigarette butts that old men garbage collectors would sweep with thinning brooms around sunrise. Clouds of conversations bumped into one another, intertwined, lost themselves among the mass. Discarded juice boxes of *Ron Planchao* rum resembled leaves flattened along the road. One boisterous boy shoved another backward into one of the boxy topiary shrubs. It bounced him back to standing as if in slow motion. He waved his arms in indignation, turned away, and disappeared into the crowd.

"We're really sad tonight, can't you tell?" Lucía shouted once I found her on a bench. "You know, Almeida and all, generals dying, time of mourning. *Vaya, vaya, vaya.*"

"Dropping like flies," said a tall guy with a pronounced pout.

A cigarette dangled from twenty-two-year-old Carlos's long fingers. He reached behind him to flick the ash to the sidewalk as he turned to look at me, leaning his cheek in for a greeting. He twisted back to the center of the group and shouted a response to whatever someone had just said. His eyes were thoughtful and calm, but the rest of him was brusque, agitated, exaggerated. The more he spoke, the faster his hands and his words flew. When I seemed confused he turned to look at me curiously down his beaky nose, and then turned, deliberate, back to the group. He and his friends, gay men who worked in theater and film, were on G Street until they headed to the weekly pop-up "Divino" LGBT party, the only activity that hadn't been cancelled in Almeida's name, because "the gays don't respect anyone's rules," Lucía said.

The apartment that his family rented was occupied by another tenant, Carlos said, but his mother knew all about the apartments for rent in their neighborhood. If I called him in a day, two days, maybe three, he'd have a few names and numbers of friends of his mother's that needed renters. He pulled my address book from my hands and wrote his phone number and name in wobbly capital letters. He pushed his black hair, a deflated Elvis 'do, out of his face. When we walked to the party, Carlos loped along the sidewalk in front of the crowd. Once at the rooftop terrace, he joined me to lean against the building's edge, thick as a concrete bench, on the opposite side from the speakers that blared muddy trance music. We nursed warm $1 beers and talked about movies, how Keira Knightley seemed always to shift between benign bewilderment and manic, open-mouthed excitement.

When we wandered the streets of Vedado and Miramar for a few hours later that week, Carlos was in no rush, since he neither worked nor studied. He wore plaid shorts and neon yellow faux Ray-Bans and stood in the doorways of places we saw with his arms crossed. But nothing fit: the three apartments were either big and expensive or, in one case, small and dark, in an enormous hulk of Soviet concrete, off the main bus and *máquina* routes. I told the smallest apartment's owner that I'd call her the next day.

As we walked back to his place, Carlos deemed me more high-maintenance than even himself. He looked shocked that such a thing was possible. *"M'ija*, estás en Cuba," he said. "You're not going to find a big, cheap, legal, centrally located apartment with a balcony. It does not exist. I don't know where you think you are but you're not in *Nueva York*—get used to it. Adjust your standards." His chiding echoed in the blue, graffitied stairwell as we climbed to his fourth-floor apartment.

We reached his floor and Carlos opened the door onto a large living room in jewel tones—magenta on the walls and lush emerald potted plants in one corner—with shiny marble floors and natural light ribboning in. His mother, Elaine, was neither rude nor discreet about looking me up and down as Carlos introduced us. She wore a green-and-yellow-plaid apron, which she removed and hung next to the stove before joining us in the living room. The dog, Carolina, trotted out behind her. The tiny black cat, which Carlos had plucked mewling from a dumpster on his way back from a party early one morning and named Oscar (de la Renta), clambered across knees and Elaine swatted at him. I spent the rest of the afternoon on sofas around the coffee table.

The Reyes family spoke with their bodies: eyebrows rising, mouths gaping with laughter, hands clapping together to demonstrate agreement or slapping the table to show dissent. There were fingers lifted to silence someone else—usually in vain—and hands shaking in the air alongside heads to emphasize a point. Elaine shook her head and clucked a "no" when anyone offered to help make another round of espresso but smiled at the edge of her sink when I cleared the coffee cups anyway.

Things I learned that afternoon: Carlos's brother, Maykel, didn't understand the northern European women who dated the black Centro Habana *santeros* downtown while they went through the rituals of initiation for Santería, and neither did Elaine, really, but she was too polite to agree with Maykel in front of someone she didn't know. Elaine had worked as a special education specialist for the state until a few years ago. While she was studying for her master's degree, she'd fallen asleep every night at the kitchen table after putting the boys to sleep. Nicolas, Carlos and Maykel's father, had been an athlete, a sharpshooter. He was thicker around the middle now, at close to fifty, than he'd been before. He reclined into the couch while everyone talked and though he spoke rarely and quietly, everyone else shut up when he did uncross his legs, lean into the group, and open his mouth. Carlos liked talking about politics, but he spoke too loudly when he got excited and Elaine clapped her hands sharply and pointed at the open windows to shut him up.

As light seeped from the evening, Elaine asked Carlos if he'd shown me the apartment at the back of theirs. She and Nicolas had turned their apartment's third bedroom and a service area into an independent flat: They'd added a terrace, a galley kitchen, and a separate entry in the eighties, and now it was a small one-bedroom apartment connected by two closed, locking doors with theirs. It had a slim living room, clean tile floors, and a wall of windows. The twenty-something Cuban girl who'd been there for two years was leaving for Milan sometime soon, going to visit the Italian boyfriend who paid her rent. She was just waiting for her passport to come through, said Elaine. No one knew if she'd return. The Reyes family didn't have a permit to rent to a foreigner—but they didn't have a permit to rent to a Cuban, either, and a German wintered in the flat upstairs and a Chilean political science student lived below without a problem. I was a *yanqui* and so my residency was more political and symbolic and thus the consequences more grave. But Elaine was willing to risk it if I was. Especially if I was staying for more than a few months. Renting was their family's only source of income, and they needed to save if they ever wanted to move out of Cuba. Elaine could ask the girl to find someplace else to stay for her final months in the country and I could pay what I'd have spent on the small, dank apartment.

From that first afternoon, Carlos's family represented what I loved about Havana: afternoons spent in debate, old-world hospitality, an apartment alive with people and the exchange of ideas, a fuzzy but definite feeling of complicity.

"Ay *m'ija*, si," said Carlos.

"It's ideal," echoed Lucía, who had just arrived to drink coffee and join the conversation.

Two days later, I moved in.

/// I'd been staying in Centro Habana, where the slam of architectural relics—brutalist, art nouveau, modern, and baroque buildings in a row—and the barrage of activity—peso snack stands, men who filled defunct lighters with fluid, gyms where I lifted weights made of old car gears—offset the overflowing trash bins, overpacked apartments, and clouds of fat flies. There, the dim streetlights snagged shadows on colonial-era moldings and buildings huddled in ocean mist that smelled more of rotting banana peels and urine than salt. Houses and apartment complexes in Miramar had pools and yards through which the sea breezes passed undisturbed, giving even the homes that were blocks from the water a hazy sense of swimming.

This modernist apartment complex didn't look like much, four blocks from the coast and set ten meters off the street behind a stand of stiff, browning palm trees and a reflecting pool with no water. Compared to the rococo mansions a few blocks farther into Miramar and the pink art deco house directly in front, Carlos's building looked brown and plain and riddled with apparent rot.

Each of the two Z-shaped buildings, pushed toward each other with a would-be garden between them, was five stories high, with deep balconies and X's made of yellowed masking tape on most of the windows. A few hens and roosters pecked around the rocks, dry leaves, and litter in the reflecting pool. The once-majestic building was Miramar in miniature, a dollhouse of prestige and poverty, history and gossip, left to encroaching decay but found in architecture textbooks on Tropical Modernism. It had been designed by the Cuban firm Bosch and Romañach in 1950 on a commission from a man named Guillermo Alonso, who may or may not have been Guillermo Alonso Pujol, vice president of Cuba under Carlos Prío. The complex was still sometimes used in architecture classes to demonstrate effective cross-ventilation.

There were two apartments on each floor off the blue stairwell and an elevator papered in curling wood-printed plastic that worked one week out of four. When it was functioning, everyone rode the lift even just to the second floor until it left a neighbor stranded inside hollering and waiting for someone handy—Nicolas or one of the other men—to pry him out. Each front door off the stairwell had a metal grate, crusted with rust or painted crisp white. Behind the grates, most doors stayed open throughout the day. Shards of arguments or TV blare bounced through the bare stairwell.

The exterior didn't match the gleaming floors in Elaine's apartment, the rich oiled wood window frames, the tall banana-leaf plants that towered over the living room couch, the bright afternoon light, the throw pillows that Elaine had stitched and then stuffed with obsolete VHS tape because the scant stuffing available was better used in bedroom pillows. The apartment had been meticulously cared for even as the building's facade crumbled. When the heat from cooking dampened the hair around Elaine's temples, she leaned against the polished aluminum countertops in her kitchen, smoking a cigarette and sipping from an espresso cup, feeling the wind blow around her face. "If there's no air in my kitchen," she often said, "there's not so much as a breeze in Havana."

Elaine was a black ponytail bobbing around the kitchen as she chopped vegetables at the aluminum counter or cleaned, or she was statuesque, sitting at the table or on the wicker love seat in the front windows, smoking a cigarette silent and still enough when she thought no one was around that the smoke rose around her face into a veil. Nicolas was always trying to get her to stop, she said nearly every time she lit a Popular, though I never heard him mention it.

They'd met in their early twenties and married after just a few months of courtship that included a first date all-night beach party out at the *playas del este* over which Elaine's father had been livid. Elaine had moved from a small city in eastern Cuba as a child when her father, an active Communist, was assigned a Party job in Havana. She grew up in La Lisa, a neighborhood to the west, in the house where her mother, father, sister, and niece still lived. It had once been graced with a yard but now smelled like what the neighbors were cooking. She'd married Nicolas, moved in with his family because there'd been no room with hers, and raised children in the rear apartment accessible from a new, separate entrance that, once Nicolas's father had died and his sister and her family moved to Miami in the Special Period, became their livelihood.

Nicolas had lived in this very apartment, which had belonged to a wealthy landowner, since his birth nearly fifty years earlier. His father had been the rich man's chauffeur. The man and his family had fled for Miami in a first surge of emigration that included nearly a quarter-million Cubans, mostly from the upper classes, who departed between 1959 and 1962. Nicolas's father, a working-class white man with more to gain than to lose from Castro's increasingly Communist reforms, stayed behind and moved into the apartment on orders from his boss. If the rich man couldn't have the flat in which he'd invested less than a decade earlier, he wanted it claimed by someone he deemed deserving. In October 1960, the government passed an Urban Reform Law that prohibited housing rentals in order to do away with owner-renter hierarchies, slumlords, and corporate rental agencies. All rental properties were expropriated and turned over to the government. A year later, another law confiscated all property that had belonged to the Cubans who'd left the country, now baptized *gusanos*, worms. Renters and squatters were allowed to buy their homes by paying rent to the government for between five and twenty years. Soon Nicolas's father owned a sprawling modern apartment.

In the years since, families had changed shape but remained in residence. Fifty years of lore floated through the blue stairwells, which were usually dark because no one paid for lightbulbs in common areas. The man downstairs had amassed too much wealth in the economic opening of the late nineties by working for a foreign company that paid in dollars as the rest of the country starved. He had to leave Cuba or face confiscation. His adult children lived there now. An old lady rocked in a chair on her balcony every day, mid-morning to night, in one of three identical house dresses; her children had left Cuba in the nineties. A younger cousin brought her food and waited to inherit the apartment. The seventy-year-old woman across the hall had fought as a teenager in the Revolution and been an intimate friend of Che Guevara's, Carlos told me—Che himself had given her this apartment. Upstairs, a parade of swarthy Latin American men entered and left one apartment in which a flirtatious art dealer lived. He sold the work of minor mid-century Cuban artists, because no work by the major ones could be taken from the country, and his wife's father, an architect and the original apartment owner, had designed the flat in which I now lived. All four floors had added a galley kitchen, a balcony, a rusted spiral staircase, and an independent entrance to the maid's quarters in the eighties. Cuban apartments divided and multiplied and contracted and changed according to necessity.

There was a time when Elaine had lived alone in the small apartment, when Nicolas traveled to compete. Nicolas had done well enough as a shooter that he'd been sent to Venezuela in the late eighties. Elaine told me one afternoon, when we were, as usual, doing not very much but getting to know one another, that Nicolas had almost stayed in Venezuela when the boys were very small. There was a daily hush around eleven in the morning, when Nicolas ran errands or fixed things down in the garage and their two sons were still asleep. I liked to work in the mornings and usually took a break to bring back the coffee cups I told Elaine I didn't need her to leave when she heard me moving around the apartment but which she set anyway, full of sweet espresso, delicately perched on the edge of my glass-topped table. We sat down to talk about who I was interviewing, about her family, about my family, about Cuba, about anything.

It was the Special Period and Nicolas had always hated living in Castro's Cuba. If he stayed, it meant leaving Elaine and abandoning his sons at least until they were eighteen, when they could leave Cuba. Athletes, who represented so much time and money invested in a sports complex that sportswriter Michael Lewis credits with having created the "highest-valued entrapped pool of human talent left on earth" in the form of Cuban baseball players, couldn't simply defect and expect to visit their sons every six months.

Cuban shooters are good, too: they medalled at the Olympics in 2004, 2008, and 2012, long after Nicolas had quit. Unlike visual artists and musicians, whose skill could be privately monetized, Cuban athletes in any of the number of sports for which the country is known—baseball, boxing, even ballet, which resembles sport as much as art—struggled only for pride, a government paycheck, and what they could make under the table from interview seekers or private clients wanting lessons. Their skill was corralled and siphoned into national glory and their homes were as crumbly as anyone else's. Even Olympic medalists did not live like generals.

So ballerinas defected, six at a time while on tour in Mexico; boxers and judo champions and soccer players slipped from the hotels where their teams stayed during competitions or qualifying tournaments and claimed another citizenship. Seven months after Hurricane Ike, during the two days preceding an Olympic qualifying soccer game for the under-twenty-three team, seven Cuban players would walk away from the Tampa Doubletree Hotel—leaving the Cuban team to lose to Honduras 2-0 with only ten total players—and claim asylum under the "wet foot, dry foot" policy: any Cuban who made it to American soil couldn't be deported. Imagine those ten players, sprinting back and forth trying to keep good face and wondering, when the game was over, if they were making the right choice, going home. The government would send them back out all the same, anyway. The Revolution's great achievements were education, health care, and sports, as the joke went; its failures were breakfast, lunch, and dinner.

Nicolas could probably have sent his family more money from abroad than what they made now but he'd have been absent, a bargain made by plenty of athletes' wives and the meaning of which Elaine did not kid herself about. She was not going to be stuck back in Havana, financially stable but alone, raising two fatherless boys in her nominal husband's sister's house while Nicolas dutifully went to Western Union every month and started over with a new wife, a new family.

But the nineties didn't unfold that way. Nicolas came back and gave up shooting, and his sister moved to Miami. Elaine quit social work, they started renting out the flat, and their joint profession now was keeping their home in order, keeping the renter in their back apartment content. Elaine and Nicolas were the sort of couple who wove a constant conversation around themselves. They were forever talking to one another, picking up a thread when he returned from running morning errands, when she finished cooking, in the afternoons when they sat in the front of the living room, in the mornings behind the closed door of their bedroom, their voices knitting near-visible intimacy. She curled her knees into her chest in the wicker garden chair in the front portico or tucked her feet beneath her. He slouched, the curve of his back fitting perfectly into the chair. Nicolas didn't talk much to anyone but Elaine. He liked to be busy: fixing anything in the apartment or building that needed it, sanding, oiling, or repainting their old furniture, errands. If they left it would be together, all of them, sometime in the near-ish future, and for Florida, not Venezuela.

Elaine had told the neighbors over coffee and cigarettes that an acquaintance in the housing authority had helped her get a special permit for me to live with them as Carlos's fiancée. Everyone in the apartment complex knew he was gay—he'd come out four years earlier—but sex or the promise of it made countless transgressions of the law at least defensible.

Still, the potential consequences of the government catching the Reyes family renting to me without a *casa particular* license rippled: It might be problematic for my Communist fairy godfather, since he'd vouched for me in the visa process, and crippling for my research, since I'd possibly be asked to leave the country; it could leave Elaine and Carlos and their family homeless, since illegal rental was grounds for confiscating the apartment.

I was instructed never to answer the doorbell or the phone due to my accented Spanish. I went further: I'd have taxis drop me off at the corner or a block away, since Cubans rarely took cabs and the woman who watched the street from her rocking chair was a permanent fixture on the building's façade. *El chivateo*, the threat of being ratted out, lurked everywhere and I hoped it would appear nowhere.

I called a few other landlords and told myself I was trying

to find someplace legal to live. But the truth was that once I'd moved in with the Reyes family, I knew that I'd never live far from them in Havana again.

/// "Hola, divino," began the man's voice on the message machine that Carlos called every Saturday night. "Tonight's party will be held at . . ." and then the theatrical voice gave an address. When it said, "I'll see you there," you believed it and so you followed the voice to the addresses of rooftops, basements, and back patios under eaves of aluminum siding. People called from living rooms in La Lisa or pay phones on Centro Habana streets or whoever's house they were at on Saturday evening, and then they boarded buses or jammed into *máquinas* heading downtown.

They walked or rode to places large enough to accommodate Havana's growing out and almost-out LGBT community: patios, rooftops, defunct concert halls, or skating rinks. I once met Carlos at a party in an empty Habana Vieja lot where a building had collapsed. Men had long since ferreted away the bricks and beams to sell to renovators on the side because you needed a specific renovator's permit to purchase concrete and bricks at the state stores. The speakers had been propped on piles of concrete rubble and when you danced you had to be careful to lift your feet high but the place's capacity had been enormous, larger than most so-called Divino parties.

The one occasion on which the party settled with regularity was a drag show every few weeks in Parque Lenin, an enormous tract of rolling hills and lush foliage twenty minutes outside town. On nights when someone big was headlining, well-organized swarms of young gay men and women gathered wherever a *máquina* could reliably be hailed and paid $12 for a ride out. Carlos splashed on aftershave and layered the two shirts he always wore to appear not quite so skinny and, one Saturday, leaned in my doorway and told me to come along. We'd meet his crew on G Street at 10:30. From the central avenue, his group, including a theater tech also named Carlos and two linguistics students, found a car that shot along the avenues out of Havana as the streetlights diminished. We wound along the dark roads of Parque Lenin until the parking lot appeared suddenly around a sharp turn, an oasis of vintage cars in a line with lanky drivers who leaned against hoods counting money. To one side, a dozen people lined up outside a door that poured red light into the dark park around the small amphitheater and showered the line with campy pop. Madonna de Cuba was headlining and the crowd was eager.

The Tropicana cabaret setup was here interpreted by a tinsel-loving set designer. Silvery stars and streamers hung from beams that held a small metal roof over the stage. A long, thin runway extended into the basin of the table-service area, where groups sat before bottles of Havana Club white rum and plates of cubed ham and cheese. Red-painted wood beams and cheap siding and the dry parkland outside and a slight smell of stale urine on the side of the room closest to the bathrooms combined to generate a vaguely gamy, 4-H Club feel, amplified by the preening groups of people not dancing in the bright light on the dance floor. The room buzzed with the firefly dramas of a group of people who know each other well, who can swap tidbits and look around and point out the subject of their gossip. Preparation for the spectacle, here, was half of the spectacle: A dozen people fluttered in and out of the bathroom area, not hiding the bare-chested men in tights applying eyeshadow, dresses on hangers behind them, from attendees who waited to use the toilet. Carlos and his friends, who wore jeans and preppy tops or sleeveless tees at their raciest, were conservative here: There were boys wearing satin bras and fake eyelashes or sequined halter tops and dark lipliner, girls in cargo shorts or sequined halters and jeans, some people who'd gotten government-funded sex change operations in the year and a half since they'd been legalized, some cross-dressers who hadn't and never would. People didn't look the same and that was the point. Ten years from now, this party's equivalent promised to be more polished, more separated into cliques.

Ten years ago, Carlos and I might have been put in jail for being at a party like this. Forty years ago, he could have been sent to a work camp for being suspected of homosexuality. "No homosexual represents the Revolution, which is a matter for men, of fists and not feathers, of courage and not trembling, of certainty and not intrigue, of creative valor and not sweet surprises," the official newspaper *El Mundo* stated in 1965. Where at the start the Revolution promised an egalitarian society that had lured support from gay Cubans, the new government quickly turned against them. The expulsion of Americans, the rehabilitation of prostitutes, the reclamation of property erected by a foreign force, and money poured into cultivating sportsmen who could do battle on the field: The Revolution was a practical but also a symbolic action, defending a conquered Cuba from the penetration and dominance of the North. Machismo was as essential to the cause as homogeneity. The University of Havana expelled gay students and the Union of Young Communists shunned men they deemed "feminine."

And yet, wrote gay Cuban writer Reinaldo Arenas, "I think that in Cuba there was never more fucking going on than in those years, the decade of the sixties, which was precisely when all the new laws against homosexuals came into being, when the persecutions started and concentration camps were opened, when the sexual act became taboo while the 'new man' was being proclaimed and masculinity exalted."

Arenas nearly died in jail after being discovered trying to smuggle his writing out. His work captures a sexually fluid Havana where any sex was understood to be better than no sex regardless of gender pairing, but where pervasive homophobia and violence and prison stints layered dark experiences and a sheen of prudishness onto the eroticism. Some members of his crowd were jailed; others were sent to Military Units to Aid Production (UMAP), the Cuban version of a gulag. Gay men were rounded up off the streets or given a false summons to their obligatory military service and hauled off to work in fields or quarries sixty hours per week for 7 pesos per month. They worked alongside practicing Roman Catholics, Jehovah's Witnesses, long-haired hippies, and "counterrevolutionaries." The UMAP program ended in 1968 but the camps remained open, paying involuntary internees slightly higher wages. Penal code revisions decreased punishments for homosexuality gradually, over the course of the seventies, eighties, and nineties.

Back then, "Neither teachers nor doctors could be gay. Today, no military person can be gay either," said Mariela Castro, gay rights activist and daughter of Raúl in an interview shortly after her father's appointment. Today, there is still no recognition of gay unions in Cuba. Same-sex couples do not hold hands in the street and gay parties and clubs are not advertised as such. But the first year of her father's presidency, 2008, saw government-funded sex change operations for transsexuals, a measure for which she'd lobbied since 2005. She promised more change, and soon.

At Parque Lenin, someone flicked up the music and a hoot rose from the burbling crowd of around a hundred and fifty, around two-thirds male, all now clapping rhythmically in anticipation. A parade of half-nude Cubans began. A sexy guerrilla fighter ripped off his army-green shirt and aviator sunglasses to show a chiseled face and rippling abs; a woman wore a modified nun's habit and a garter belt; a goth girl, in fishnets, high boots, bra, and cape, whipped her long black hair like a flag as she spun around. They retreated, flushed and bouncing their way into a cluster to the side of the stage, as the variety show started. A tall transvestite threw her arms out wide while lip-synching to "The Diva Dance," the blue alien aria from *The Fifth Element*. A purple-clad drag queen with inch-long talons on delicate hands pounded her chest a la Celine Dion as she faux-sang Cher. Someone did a rousing dance to a Gloria Trevi song. Carlos sang along quietly. Between acts, two men in boxer-briefs pulled a red curtain open and closed. During performances, they stood statuesque on either side of the stage.

There was a pause. The stage cleared and the crowd stared at the curtain, where the two men stood with bunched handfuls of fabric in their hands, at the ready to sprint clumsily backward and reveal Madonna strung up on a silver cross papered with aluminum foil. A roar rolled through the room. She was tall with a chin cleft and red lips. Long blond hair hung over cleavage that spilled from a black pleather bustier. She began with "Like a Prayer," mouthing the intro words. When the beat line kicked in, she leapt from the cross and roamed the stage. She clasped her hands together (*like a little prayer*), dropped to the floor (*down on my knees*), pointed to the audience (*want to take you there*), and then up at the open sky that winked into the amphitheater. She dropped again to the floor and vogued, her legs scissoring through the air.

The crowd around her wasn't gossiping anymore. The collective craving for spectacle, for someone to part the curtain and emerge, confident and with a hip swagger and an arm flourish and a presence as different as humanly possible from everyone who walked down G Street at four in the afternoon—that craving had been recognized and met. This entire room was in varying stages of standing out. No one leaned into bathroom mirrors applying eye shadow in order to fit into the Cuban crowd. And indeed, when more permits were given to open private in-home bars in 2011, a drag bar lined in synthetic velvet brought into the country in checked suitcases would open on the outskirts of town. On the two nights that I would go with Carlos, the performers would outnumber their audience but, with consummate professionalism, put on a show with verve and sequins just the same, and the two of us would clap and dance wildly alone on the dance floor. Carlos's arms were a barometer of his emotional state: when he was happy, he carved a radius around himself. He walked with his arms swinging; he pulled me into a casual hug; he danced with slow, broad movements that delineated the bubble of his reach. Whenever Carlos danced at gay parties late at night, his arms moved gracefully and around a wide personal perimeter.

Madonna left the stage to two standing ovations. As had become our routine, I left the party earlier than Carlos. He would stay at Parque Lenin until the party ended around four, and then he would sit in the kitchen to watch TV for a few hours. Nicolas had stretched an antenna out of the kitchen window to catch a cable signal from the state-run hotel across the street. The TV got shadowy, staticky CNN *en español*, Showtime, and a few local southern Florida channels, since the satellites thought they were beaming to an account in the Keys. Carlos sat in a stiff wooden chair, eating bread with mayonnaise or leftover rice and beans in the bluish glow of "Law & Order: SVU" and reality TV reruns until his eyes began to slip closed.

Elaine had never been to a drag show at Parque Lenin.

But her son's homosexuality didn't bother her, she said. It was his lack of goals that worried her. Going to social gatherings was his only aspiration, and lately, he'd been going primarily to gay parties. Elaine was afraid that as Carlos sank his identity into this one community, this one aspect of who he was, he did so at the expense of the other aspects of his personality: his intellect, his drive to debate, his passion for art and cinema. Even his strong opinions, his outspoken nature, his curiosity. All things he could use to make a life for himself if he wanted to. He had never found any motivation, she said. This was part of why she had finally agreed to leave Cuba.

The Reyes family's appointment at the U.S. Interests Section, the euphemistic name that the U.S. government has used since its embassy was shuttered in 1961, was scheduled for April 2011. A year from the coming April, they'd hand in their papers and meet with a representative of the government that they hoped to call their government, and fingers were crossed that they'd be given Family Reunification Visas, since they'd been sponsored by Nicolas's sister in Miami. They'd do their best to convince interviewers that they were ideal Cuban Americans, industrious and family-oriented just like so many of the families that had settled among the billboards and smooth asphalt and trim watered lawns of southern Florida.

This was why Elaine risked renting to me—as a *yanqui*, I paid more than a Cuban would, more even than a German, and she and Nicolas needed to save. Their family was sponsoring them in the eyes of the government, but Elaine and Nicolas had to foot the departure bill themselves: four passports, medical checkups, exit visas, entry visas, plane tickets, and at least some startup capital. Until April 2011, their lives were dominated by a tight-belted routine, their bubble of stasis defined at its edges by the specter of a life, together, that all were envisioning slightly differently but none could imagine.

/// Every aisle of a state supermarket, *la chopin*, held variations on a theme: aisle one, Herdez canned peas, beets, and four sorts of dark-meat tuna; on two, Canadian corn flakes and Chinese noodles and every imaginable shape of Barilla pasta; three, Tetra Pak milk and Pomi tomatoes; four, an entire aisle of Brazilian cookies in metallic packages, wafers and biscuits and off-brand Oreos; five, all-purpose cleaning products in varying scents, an army of bottles emblazoned with cartoonish gleaming floors glowering down. Most *agromercados*, the agriculture markets where anything that can be grown in Cuba is sold in local pesos, stocked plantains and tiny bananas and yucca and a few wilting heads of cabbage. There was one *agro* downtown where piles of bright fresh peppers and firm guavas and the occasional lush head of lettuce were sold at slight markups to those who could pay more, expats and people with family abroad and those who ran *casas* or in-home restaurants.

Elaine rarely resorted to going to that *agro*. Too expensive. And somehow she set inexpensive feasts before her family every day at lunchtime. *Ropa vieja*, the classic Cuban beef dish; pillowy *tortilla española* with potato, green pepper, and onion; chicken drumsticks with tomato sauce.

A photographer friend of mine, Juan, passed along the number of a man he knew who sold food on the black market. The day I called him, he had bacon, Serrano ham, blue cheese, parmesan, wines, and olive oil, though at later dates he'd also have smoked salmon and mozzarella, too. I placed my order and he said he'd be over in the morning.

The next morning I waited at my window. When I saw

the person I assumed was him parking a tinny scooter in the lot, I leaned out of the building's shadow and called his name softly. He was a thirty-something man with a serious expression and abundantly gelled hair. I pointed at the rickety spiral staircase at the back. Bottles clacked against one another as he lugged them up the two flights to my apartment.

I poured him a glass of cool water as he pulled out the items I'd asked for. He set them on my glass-topped table. Two bottles of Chilean Cabernet Sauvignon that retailed for $9 in the state stores, two for $10 from him. One liter of satisfying, green olive oil, $9. A four-pound bag of grated parmesan cheese. And a shrink-wrapped haunch of cured Serrano ham the size of a small child. Fifteen pounds.

I looked on with awe, glee, and confusion. "Great. How are we going to cut this?"

"You said you wanted Serrano," he said quickly, pulling out a two-inch thick wad of CUC and licking a fingertip. "If you'd told me you wanted a half of a *jamón Serrano*, maybe I could have found another client who wanted to split this one and delivered half and half, but it's too late for that now. If you don't want it, I'll find someone else."

"But what am I going to do with all of this?" I waved my arms vaguely, as if trying to help him see how big the ham looked to me in my small space.

"*Mira*, what most of my clients do, they go to one of the supermarkets and they give the guy behind the meat counter a dollar or two to slice it really thin on the machine," he said.

I retreated to my bedroom to see if the only American expatriate I knew in Havana wanted half; I called Juan and he committed to a chunk. Back in my living room, I handed the vendor $70, cleared out the bottom half of my refrigerator, and locked the door behind him.

"Next time, *hija*, you have to be specific," Elaine said sternly.

"Ask prices, sizes, weights, everything. Next time order an extra olive oil for me and I'll leave you the money—the doctor says I need it for my cholesterol. Now, if you will, give me a tiny hunk of that fat and I'll bring you a *tupper* of the stew I'm making."

Elaine bought nearly nothing from the state stores, where Canadian cornflakes sold for $12 and olive oil for $14. Items that she regularly purchased through technically illegal venues included cheese, eggs, fish (both fresh and frozen), tomato paste, yogurt, coffee, horse meat (killing a cow merited a jail sentence, since beef was scarce and earmarked for state supermarkets; horse meat, gamier and tougher, substituted well in *ropa vieja*), wine (when there was money for it, which was rare), clothing, acetone for removing nail polish, pots and pans, and diesel fuel for the car her younger son sometimes rented from a neighbor to use as a gypsy cab on weekend nights. Communist Party officials with state cars sold whatever they didn't use of their rationed gas and diesel. Employees at all-inclusive hotels filched wine, olive oil, cheeses, prosciutto, and more from storerooms to sell via an immense web of contacts. And ever since the 2008 hurricane season, when customs taxes for bringing food into Cuba were eliminated to help families recover from Ike, awkward suitcases had brought in the stock for black-market vendors' itinerant shops.

Scenes of everyday domestic life included the egg man standing outside the door with an improbable plastic bucket of fragile eggs that never seemed to break in transit. Once cracked, they revealed bright yellow yolks. Every month or so, there was the woman who stopped by with a rolling suitcase filled with Zara pants and cheap men's briefs that she spread on Elaine's dining room table after ferrying them in lumpy checked suitcases from Panama. There was a white sateen tablecloth that appeared on my kitchen table around five in the afternoon on the first day that I invited someone over for dinner. Every time I had guests, the tablecloth materialized.

There was Nicolas hefting sacks of rice and sugar onto the kitchen counter, having returned from the *bodega*, the ration shop, with little else, despite the fact that the unbleached pages of paper promised a long list of items that were rarely available: grains, oil, refined sugar, raw sugar, baby food, bath soap, washing soap, toothpaste, salt, coffee, and cigarettes, signed and stamped after each dispensed serving. Pages detailed specially prescribed medical diets and age categories that Elaine's family didn't fall into: extra meat, chicken, root vegetables. For car owners, gas. For children, fish, milk, eggs, soy yogurt, and, when they were available, yearly balloons and cakes for birthday parties. But these items were rarely available at their *bodega*, for no reason other than "por que la leche es hasta los siete años," because you get milk until you're seven years old, slang for "Lord only knows." The *bodega* food was usually bad: broken rice with bits of chaff and gravel that required grain-by-grain sorting on the kitchen table, stringy chicken or pork when there was any, small black beans that worked out to a few pots' worth. But Elaine made do: She used the chicken in stews that camouflaged its quality, bodega rice in yellow pilaf with hot dogs, beans in wet cumin-scented side dishes alongside *ropa vieja*, meals that lived between the state-sanctioned and the black markets.

Every morning, she spent hours preparing the big family lunch, buying root vegetables and cabbage and tomato from the cheapest *agro* in the area, soaking plantains for *tostones*, slicing cucumbers and cabbage and tomato for salad, sorting beans and boiling oil and sautéing peppers. Soon enough, after eating lunch with them nearly every day and helping Elaine in order to learn her recipes, I had to remember to tell her sometime before ten if she shouldn't set five placemats at the table. She wasn't a master chef—her dishes were simple, Cuban staples, well-executed with spice and proportion—but she cared. Good food required time and effort and creativity, but it was a daily rebuke to the utilitarianism of the regime, a private nod to the pleasure principle. Eating well in Havana was thrilling for its rarity and subversive in its luxury.

Every morning, I opened the door onto the two-meter-square patio at the very rear of the apartment complex and looked at the familiar skyline of downtown Vedado, the turquoise Riviera Hotel, and further, the indistinct hulk of the Focsa apartment building. I had bought a small fern to put in the corner, which quickly became, as Elaine had said it would, thin from the northern winds that whipped through in the fall. There were trees out back: a lime tree, coconut palms, and a mango tree that mostly hid the garages made of patchwork aluminum siding in the middle of the block. Behind the garages, a few rusty oil barrels, the exoskeleton of a car, chunks of tile piled high, to be used as a mosaic floor in the never-ending renovation of the house next door.

Domesticity constructed a new Havana, a city of routine and immediacy and absurdity.

I walk into the kitchen one afternoon and Elaine and Nicolas are on the floor, butts in the air, miniature skyscrapers of plates in a disorganized suburb around their bodies as they reach deep into the back of the cabinets to clean. "I found a tiny cockroach," Elaine says, not disgusted but surprised, almost gleeful, vindicated. Nicolas grunts and lumbers past me to the maid's area sink to wet the towel he's using to swipe surfaces that had never looked dirty to begin with.

My toilet breaks. The arm that runs from flush to chain is broken and I reach into the water, up to my elbows, to flush the toilet. After a day or two of waiting, why I don't know, I tell Nicolas and spend an afternoon out of the house and when I come back the top is still off the toilet. Nicolas hears me enter when the rusty grate over my back entrance sings and he follows me to the bathroom to show me: he's melted a Bic pen over the open burner so it mimics the shape of the broken metal arm. He gleams as I coo at his ingenuity. The back end is screwed just tight enough to grip the metal chain. It works for a few days and then the chain slips off and keeps slipping off and though I reach into the toilet to fix it, reduce to every-other-time flushing because I'm taken with the aesthetic of flushing my Cuban toilet with a melted Bic pen, it gets old. Again, I tell Nicolas, hesitantly this time, and he nods. He spends a day trying to find a metal arm, riding around in *máquinas* and, by nightfall, he's found one, and my toilet is fixed, but something is lost, too.

Elaine brings me coffee in the morning the way she does. She high-steps like a cheerleader across the six-inch threshold with a teacup full of sludgy coffee—now with half the amount of sugar that Cubans usually use, how I like it—and today she has the cordless phone in her hand. "*Hija*, if it rings, answer it. Tell whoever it is that I'll call them back. I have to go out. There are no sanitary napkins at the stores near here and the bodega has only loose cotton and it's at this point an emergency." She's hitching a ride with the upstairs neighbors, the wealthy art dealer couple, who are driving around to all of the grocery stores on a loop, the weekly run to see what's where. She doesn't know when she'll be back.

There is no toilet paper at any of the stores I've been to and I have two rolls left. Elaine tells me about the tiny shop inside the tourist complex ten blocks from our house, Le Select, which is too small to be a regular stop on the food circuit. I buy six four-packs, which join the pantry that is creeping along shelves and into my closets. A few weeks later, I hear from an Italian businessman that the shortage is due to rising shipping costs.

Cuba imported boatloads of paper scraps from Canada to make its toilet paper, he said. The government hadn't paid the shipping company in a while, so the paper delivery had halted.

/// Carlos decided to apply to college. There was one thing that could keep him in Cuba for a while longer, he told me one afternoon as I sat at my dining table and he, as usual, leaned lankily against the doorjamb between our two apartments, smoking a cigarette: a film degree. Now that people he knew were actually leaving for the rest of the world, many of them armed with degrees and at least some fluency in another language, the gaping possibility of poverty in the world abroad opened wide and dark before him. He spoke little English; he had no training, no degree, no skills. He had never even waited a table or washed a floor. Carlos was smart and passionate and confident, but what else?

Carlos had taken the college entrance exams once before, right after high school. With the help of a psychiatrist friend of his mother's, he'd been excused from the mandatory military service that all Cuban males completed after high school because of a nervous personality disorder with which he'd been diagnosed. The University of Havana awaited him, he knew it, and he'd requested art history or sociology or communications when he took the exam. But his scores on the "Cuban History" part—which everyone knew was just a way of testing how well you could parrot propaganda—had been too low. He was offered a spot in pharmacology, dentistry, or nutritional studies; all occupations, since they were medical careers, that would complicate his ability to acquire an exit visa when the time came. Besides, they bored him. So he took a short course in theater production that Elaine had paid extra to get him into but quit. He spent three years doing nearly nothing but the occasional favor for a friend-of-a-friend.

Two friends would take the exam, too, and they gathered every afternoon at Elaine's dining room table for three weeks with books and study guides and a laptop on which they'd saved documentation about the tests of years past. They would be tested on art history, architecture, literature, world history, and film.

"Por dios," Elaine flushed in the doorway between our apartments the first week. "This boy expects me to feed everyone. Come help me; I want to make that chicken thing you make with the chili you brought from Mexico. We'll use up what chicken I have and I'll tell him tomorrow that this won't do."

I followed her and we cooked dinner silently, listening to the conversation from the other room. "No, no, that's new wave, not noir." Carlos was twitchy with adrenaline, pacing back and forth and drinking the glasses of water that Elaine reminded him to drink. Elaine tried unsuccessfully to hide her emotions: content approval that he had a goal, worried about what that goal meant for her family's emigration plans. She cooked for his group two more times before the exams took place.

3

JUST HAIR

LIVÁN

By the numbers, G Street is the biggest party in Havana, and not just on nights when generals die. Thursday through Sunday, people perch on the benches, which have splintery green wooden slats, and drink from boxes of rum in the park-like patches of dry grass between the median's central promenade and the sidewalk. Dozens stand on corners in loose circles that, in time, grow amorphously into the street. When this happens, drivers honk horns and policemen shuffle toward them and the kids retreat to the sidewalk.

I met Liván, Takeshi, and the rest of their photogenic band of *frikis*—rock and metal fans of the punk-and-anarchist subcategory—around nine on a Thursday night. They loped down the hill with long arms swinging, four in front, and then three, weaving through the clusters of people in their way, pushing each other into onlookers. Their clothes were a mid-nineties punk-grunge hodgepodge: torn jeans, wallet chains, boots, scruffy Converse shoes, inked limbs. Each had sculpted his hair into a Mohawk or some variation on it. They strove to take up space.

The acquaintance I was with snapped a candid shot of one of the *frikis* from the side, and when they all turned around, he asked if he could take a few pictures. They consented with shrugs. He shot each of the boys in sequence as they heckled one another and I sat down on a bench nearby. The camera's flash made the shiny leaves of the bushes in the background gleam along with the studs in the boys' lips, eyebrows, noses, and ears. One boy being photographed wore a somber-looking expression that, momentarily, evaporated to reveal an eager smile. Then he pressed his lips together again. Liván stood next to me in a white T-shirt with fuzzy neon polka dots spray-painted on it.

"So, what kind of music do you listen to?" I asked no one in particular.

"*Poooooonk,*" a different voice shouted from three feet away as Liván opened his mouth.

"I love Joe Strummer," I said.

Liván sat down. His face was blank.

"From the Clash," I clarified, too loudly.

Recognition sparked, and Liván grinned. "Us, too," he said. He introduced himself and the boy who'd just sat down next to him, Takeshi, whose nickname came from a Japanese manga character that he apparently resembled.

"*Los Ramo-nays,* too," added Takeshi.

Liván's hair was twisted into about a dozen six-inch spikes that extended directly out from his head like a fragile medieval mace. "*Asere,* he looks like a pineapple," one of the boys crowed when I asked how long it had taken him to construct. I laughed and then saw that they looked at me expectantly. "Nah, it looks cool," I said. Another shouted, "Yeah, that's it, looks so cool they'll send a boat from Miami to come get you!" They snickered.

They answered questions in unison: Where did they live (*far away*), what had they done that night (*gone to Maxim Rock for a concert, but the sound system was broken and they didn't have cash for the cover anyway*), what were they doing for the rest of the night (*G Street*). Takeshi's bony shoulders slouched forward as he sat, and the red printed words on the front of his black T-shirt gaped and billowed, indistinct. He drummed his fingers on his knees, tapping the rhythm of a phantom song, and the spikes on his cuff thumped against his jeans. His face was fine-boned and handsome, with deep-set dark eyes and an aquiline nose and full lips. He said he was seventeen, looked about twelve, and turned out to be fifteen. He flashed me his ID to prove his age.

Where they had seemed sharp-edged before opening their mouths, they softened, puppy-like, after a few minutes of talking. We hung out on G for half an hour or so, and I asked if I could go to a concert with them over the weekend. I'd been to a few metal shows when I'd lived in Havana in college, I told them, and I wondered if it was any different now. Takeshi told me to meet them on Saturday at Liván's house around four or five in the afternoon. We'd go from there.

"You gotta see his room," he said, with a knowing glance at Liván.

"Yeah," a few of the boys who'd circled around us murmured. "Totally."

Liván nodded. "I guess it's pretty radical."

They wrote the address and phone number in my worn notebook and ambled down the avenue.

/// Isolation is intrinsic to Havana. For those without a government desk job, email is checked at hotels, where an hour on slow and sometimes out-of-service Internet costs about $8. Cards to access wifi signals in hotel lobbies, a bit more expensive, are usually in stock only at whichever hotel you've chosen not to go to, as the indifferent women at the desks say while pointing you toward the exit without meeting your gaze. Prepaid cell phones cost 50 cents a minute for both outgoing and incoming calls—most people can't keep them charged with money and use them as pagers. Shared *fijos* at *casas* are often tied up.

G Street is a product of this isolation and an unstated will to combat it. During the day, it's a central avenue in downtown Havana with firm topiary hedges, monuments to dead heroes, and curbs painted with strict black-and-white stripes, a Tim Burton–esque flourish in the fecund tropics, all sloping gently down to the ocean. Little distinguishes it from any of Havana's wide, Paris-on-the-sea boulevards—this area of the city was, in fact, designed in the twenties by French landscape architect J. C. N. Forestier. Colonnaded mansions are set back behind semicircular driveways and rich tropical trees, and on main streets, the government keeps them freshly painted in bright tones of yellow and pink and red that fade to ecru and rose as the sun sets.

On Thursday, Friday, and Saturday nights, Havanans mostly between the ages of thirteen and thirty eat their dinners at home, shed their school or, if they're older, work uniforms, don the clothes that are like passwords for whatever subculture they belong to, and flock to Calle G. At what quickly begins to resemble a massive outdoor house party, they mill in clusters, lounge on benches, and sit on the sidewalk amid blobs of discarded gum and cigarette butts, their knees crooked in upside-down *V*'s in front of them. Smoke hangs in the air even when there's a breeze. Most usually stay until three or four in the morning. Some stick around until sunrise doing what looks like nothing all night long. Every so often, rumors spread that policemen will show up on a Friday night and round everyone up under the charge of "social dangerousness" or "a pre-criminal danger to society," hazy Cuban legal terms that carry with them up to four years in prison.

Even if it's only symbolic and really quite tenuous, G Street is the sliver of Havana that belongs to young Cubans—not to their families, like their crowded apartments, and not to the government, like concert spaces and cafés and basically everywhere else. And it's free. The people on G Street spend what cash they have on tangible goods, clothing and accessories and cell phones. Wearing brand names is a small, silent "up yours" to the Revolution's goals of non-materialism and equality—Ed Hardy, Nike, and Tommy Hilfiger labels as tightly curled fists against the drab green canvas of identical bureaucrats. The crowd teems under impotent machetes lofted by the statues of patriots on every block.

The *friki* were the ones who had initially colonized G Street a few years earlier. They'd had to: El Patio de Maria, heavy metal's only consistent concert venue and gathering spot, was shut down in 2003 amid rumors of drug use. Malicious stereotyping, said every *friki* I spoke with, each of whom spouted conspiracy theories about how the government just didn't want the rockers to get any more popular.

Rock had been frowned upon in Cuba since the Revolution swept out mafiosos, Coca-Cola, and anything that sounded like Elvis. The philosophical roots of the Cuban Revolution lay not only in Marxism but in Latin American national liberation movements; the arts were the front line, wrote Minister of Culture Armando Hart Dávalos, of the "political, social and moral development of the society." Music in English was forbidden. Even as the government has insisted that Beatles fandom was never really a punishable offense, urban legends of listening to the Fab Four in secret shortly after the Revolution abound.

The Ministry of Culture required that radio stations play Cuban music 70 percent of the time. Still, children of the new Communist Party leadership begged their parents to bring back Rolling Stones vinyls from trips abroad through the sixties and seventies. Records circulated surreptitiously, as long as the police who raided the Coppelia ice cream parlor hippie hangout to search for "homosexuals and anti-patriotic dissidents" couldn't find them in the young adults' macramé bags. By the late sixties, guitar-strumming twenty-somethings Silvio Rodríguez and Pablo Milanés were growing famous for socially conscious anthems, to the chagrin of ministry leadership, who saw only their resemblance to the American folk movement. But the lyrics were fiery and Communist, and the Casa de las Américas cultural center director, respected revolutionary Haydée Santamaría, supported the musicians— opposition quietly subsided. The music was christened *la nueva trova*, and it would dominate the public sphere throughout the seventies and eighties. That one of the genre's main influences was rock and folk rock from the United States and Britain was not discussed.

When a few bands began to openly play rock in the eighties and early nineties, the music genres had compressed: Strains that were sharply delineated outside Cuba (punk, metal, rock, grunge) lumped together into a loud, guitar-and-drum-based sound with subversive undertones. The police trained their eyes on the *friki*'s hangouts. Not only was rock still the musical ambassador of the enemy, but the local fan base didn't have money to spend on CDs or entry fees. The *frikis* were, as Cuban writer and rock singer Yoss wrote, "distinguished by their dress and attitude: 'We're bad cuz nobody loves us; nobody loves us 'cuz we're bad.'"

Within this vacuum, rock trudged along. El Patio de Maria opened and state venues occasionally gave the bigger bands—Zeus, Metal Oscuro—a slot. The small regional festivals that had tried for footholds before the Special Period found renewed support in the provinces. Bands, punk and metal and grunge, blossomed: Porno Para Ricardo, Tendencia, Venus, more. Rock had a scene in the nineties. It was small, but it was a scene nonetheless. Then El Patio de Maria shuttered. With nowhere else to go downtown—the wide spots of the *malecón* were the province of hustlers on one end and the gay scene on the other—the Mohawked *friki* headed to G Street. Even when rock was recognized in officialdom via the creation of the Agencia Cubana de Rock, a splinter organization within the Union of Young Communists, G Street remained the hub. Official rock seemed a Frankenstein music genre.

Within a few years, G Street had become the epicenter of Havana's teenagers and young adults, the place for people who traced firm differences between themselves and what appeared on *telenovelas* or the people who went to the official P.M.M. ("Por un Mundo Mejor," For a Better World) shows, thrown by government nightlife promoters.

Groups on G Street are differentiated mostly by the details of their sartorial choices and what kind of music comes out of the speakers on the cell phones that they don't have money to use for calls. There is a hardly visible but serious line between the *mikis*, the hipsters, and the *profundos*, the intellectual hippie-bohemians who often wear the same jeans and Converse, but listen to Silvio Rodríguez and Bob Dylan and accessorize with knit purses instead of fake Coach. The *friki*, identifiable by long hair, black clothing, piercings, and tattoos, are not the *emo*, who wear black and pink clothes, bangs like curtains across their eyes, and raccoon-circle eyeliner, and both hate the *repa(rteros)*, who come from Havana's *repartos* or poorer neighborhoods, listen to *timba* groups and some reggaeton, and wear anything brand-name.

Uniform poverty gave every choice of self-presentation meaning and commitment. Real Nikes or fake, red or black nail polish, tight jeans or looser ones, hair worn in a single long braid or half-back and puffed up in front with bobby pins, music in Spanish or English or perhaps Italian. The groups on G Street offered a genealogical map of youth culture in Havana for anyone with the stamina to study it.

/// Liván lived on a plain street in La Lisa. Getting there required either a long wait for a heaving bus or the good fortune of hailing a *máquina* headed that way from downtown. What was usually a flat ten-peso charge for a ride along Havana's main avenues in patchwork old vehicles of the Chevy-Studebaker persuasion doubled on journeys to the outer boroughs. These long trips funneled Havana into a tiny village: talkative strangers traded news, baseball scores, and shopping tips, and acquaintances who traveled the same routes hopped in and out of back seats.

Decades ago, Communist Party officials like Elaine's father had asked for homes in La Lisa, because it was there that they could sow vegetable gardens and enjoy fresh air. But most of those yards had since filled in with ramshackle home additions and the neighborhood had sprouted colonies of squatters. By the time I met Liván, a common way to say, "I'm screwed" in local jargon was "I'll have to live under the bridge to La Lisa."

Liván's street was a ten-minute walk up a slight incline from the main road, in the nicer half of the neighborhood. The sidewalks were laced with grass and the street's potholes were speed bumps for the few cars that bounced by. The odd wood-frame house, one every block or two, looked rickety and impermanent amid the faded pastel concrete of the others. In the occasional undeveloped lots, ferns, palms, and banana leaf trees grew in a riot and bougainvilleas clambered around undulating chicken-wire fences. These lots, combined with the sound of chirping birds, gave La Lisa an indistinct countryside feeling, a vestige of what the neighborhood must once have been.

It was mid-afternoon and the pungent scent of coffee emerged from doors and windows. The monotone singsong of a man peddling itinerant repair services—"re-pa-ra-ciones ma-quinas de gaaas"—echoed from a few streets over. As I turned onto Liván's street, growling tones of heavy metal began to crescendo. Liván's mother leaned against the rail of her porch smoking a cigarette. She smiled and nodded, kissed my cheek, shouted "Bertha," and gestured to herself. Her grin revealed that she had very few teeth. She waved me inside.

Hers was the same single-story, shotgun-style home that could be seen all over Cuba: entry living room, narrow hallway, two bedrooms with a bathroom between them in the center, and a kitchen and dining-room area in the back. Small patios bookended the house. The front living room held two wooden benches, a shelf with a few books on it, a stereo, a TV, a WWF poster of Stone Cold Steve Austin and a photo of Liván and three of his brothers, blond and angelic in matching white T-shirts. Down the hallway, the same group of kids who'd gathered on Thursday smoked cigarettes around the doorway of Liván's room.

He had papered and painted the walls and ceiling of his bedroom with images and words: a Cypress Hill poster and one of a droll *telenovela* heartthrob named Maite; a Nickelodeon image of a grinning, greenish SpongeBob SquarePants; a Cuban flag with a punk manifesto scrawled on it; multiple photos of Che Guevara. Liván had written a marginally coherent rant in block letters six inches high: "To be punk is a form of life not only a type of music. I am punk, I vent my aggression at Che and reggaeton and if you don't like it go to 23 and G because there's nothing else to do here." On another wall, he'd painted symbols in finger-thick yellow paint:

$$ \dagger = \text{卐} = \text{☭} $$

On all four walls, he had pasted sixteen fines he'd been given by policemen, small white sheets of paper scrawled on with handwriting so similar they could have been written by the same person on different days. Disorderly conduct, talking back to policemen, being in public without identification. Each offense carried with it a fine of seven to thirty pesos, all unpaid. In the far corner of the room, the lumpy mattress he shared with a younger brother wore thin flowered sheets.

Liván and two others boys watched Takeshi fix another kid's hair in the bathroom. Takeshi stood on the toilet bowl to get a better angle. His brow was furrowed and his skinny arms moved gracefully around the crown of the other boy's head. He held them in a first-position circle that haloed the green leaves on the printed plastic shower curtain in the background. As I poked my head in, he flashed me a grin and told me to wait in the living room to see the finished product. They used soap, the kind that their mothers got on the family ration book, because gel was only sold in *la chopin* and none of them had enough CUC to buy it.

The eldest of the crew was the only one of them who worked. Erlán, whose bulging mid-section and music taste (he liked the Doors, the Grateful Dead, and AC/DC) gave away the solid decade he had on the others, cut hair in Centro Habana. He was twenty-six and had a young son, he told me later, but he didn't see the boy or his mother often.

Bertha pulled me aside to ask me how far away Kansas

City was from Oregon, where I'd told her I was from. In her hands she held an envelope of photographs in a grease-stained Walmart envelope. "Pretty far," I answered. Why did she ask? Her eldest son lived in Kansas City. She pulled out the stack of pictures and showed me photos of him, a stockier, darker version of Liván: his arm around a young woman in a kitchen; smiling next to a package of hot dogs, a few red, juicy steaks, and a grill; in a field of sparse snow, his arms extended wide; with a handful of snow, his tongue stuck out toward it and face scrunched up. Were phone calls cheap up there? Could she give me his phone number so I could call him and tell him I'd seen her and Liván? Or give him mine? "Sure," I said, and we traded numbers.

We left after they had plied each other's hair into spikes that would begin to flake white within the hour and, as the evening wore on, droop low over their ears like leaves of a too-ripe vegetable. As I followed them out of the house, saying good-bye to Bertha, she ducked in toward me. "Their thing is just hair, you know, nothing more," she said, shaking her head. Their jeans were dirty and torn but their shirts were clean, fresh-smelling.

Erlán jangled as we walked the ten blocks down the street to the bus stop. He had made a wallet chain out of beer and soda tabs he'd linked together. Since the government shops didn't sell much along the lines of their punk-y tastes, he explained, the boys made do. See Takeshi? Takeshi had bought his heavy boots from an electrician and added spikes and studs that he'd pried off a bracelet a foreigner had given him. They swapped clothes among themselves, bought at the peso shops where second, third, and fourth-hand clothing was resold, or offered government workers cash for the rationed items that they'd be issued every few years. If they saw a guy in an old Metallica T-shirt, they'd offer him a few CUC for it.

A boy named Alejandro with an eight-inch tattoo on his shaved skull wore a T-shirt that read, "Carthage College Greek Week 1997. Paint the town Greek!" with lambdas and deltas floating around it. He had spray-painted it with black and pink dots, torn the bottom hem, and drawn anarchy symbols and "Punk Not Dead" in English across the back. I pictured him crouched on the tile floor of a cramped downtown apartment, stretching the fabric taut to write on it with a Sharpie.

The bus stop cleared out as we arrived. A bus pulled up and we climbed on, but no one paid; all the boys shouldered brusquely through the standing passengers at the front to the open seats. The one girlfriend who'd been at Liván's house, a grinning sixteen-year-old with braces, had left and I was the only female present. A teenage girl and a middle-aged woman shrank back from the group as if the quills of the boys' hair were sharp.

We got off the bus and walked uphill. As we neared the amphitheater, a muddy, blaring noise grew louder. I walked toward the swooping bandshell, splotched with mold and surrounded by a tall fence, but Takeshi grabbed my arm. The boys had literally not a cent on them, he told me, so they had to scheme. We sat on the curb.

As I reached up to pass Liván a cigarette, I got a good look at the tattoo on his knuckles. A-N-A-R-Q-U-I-A, one letter on each finger to spell the word when he held his hands in fists together. It looked homemade but had cost him 5 CUC—he had gone to a black-market tattoo parlor to get it.

"There's not much you can do about anarchy here, but once I was hauled off to a police station for throwing a bottle at a cop car," he said. "It's like the Clash says: I can study, but it's for nothing, because it doesn't help me in life or to make any money or any anything." Liván had spent the three years since he'd dropped out of school at age fourteen doing not very much.

What were his goals? I asked gingerly. He looked away. He wanted to leave Cuba, he guessed. Go to Kansas, maybe, join his older brother.

And then?

He shrugged and looked away. "I don't know, anything, whatever. Aren't there punks there?"

"Hey, so," Takeshi jumped in. Would I pay for two extra entrance fees? It was 20 Cuban pesos, just shy of a dollar per person. Sure, I said. Ten minutes later, we had regrouped. Three of the boys had talked their way in and two had snuck in via a back entrance. Around a hundred and fifty kids had converged, but how many viewers had paid was unclear. A band, Hipnosis, was setting up.

When they began to play rough, monotone guitar riffs, the pink and purple lights on stage created a dissonant bubblegum effect. All around me, sweat flew from the headbanging. Takeshi emerged from the crowd and handed me a cup of rum, smuggled in by a friend of a friend. When it was over, we headed to the street and waited for a bus to take us to G. It was around ten at night.

Liván was woefully drunk from rum he'd gulped out of other people's bottles. I asked him if he'd rather just go home, and he shook his head emphatically, cartoonishly. "If my mom sees me like this, she'll kill me," he slurred. "She won't let me out of the house for a week." He swayed off to another bus shelter a few yards away to make himself sick and carry on.

Takeshi sat down with me. He'd heard me asking Liván about goals, he said. "Wanna hear mine?" he asked earnestly. "Find my *media naranja*, my soul mate, and settle down. Might as well find a woman and treat her right. As long as she likes punk. I dumped my last girlfriend; she liked *fusión* and *miki* music."

After half an hour or so, an off-duty school bus stopped. He was going as far as an intersection a mile from Twenty-Third and G, the driver shouted as he cranked open the door, and the two dozen kids who'd gathered at the bus stop whooped and pushed inside.

/// In a 1977 essay, music critic Lester Bangs wrote that "the roots of punk was the first time a kid ended up living with his parents till he was 40. The roots of punk was the first time you stole money out of your mother's purse and didn't know what to spend it on because you weren't old enough to buy beer . . . Punk is stupid proud consumerism. Punk is oblivion when it isn't any fun and unlike winos you do have a choice in fact; you're young." Okay, then. By Bangs's estimation, nearly everyone on G Street was a punk. And there were invisible punks in other pockets of the city, too, kids who'd dropped out of school or government jobs, who hand-washed crappy Brazilian imported T-shirts with logos they didn't understand in buckets in the sink and sat around their parents' houses all day long until, at night, they lined up outside a neighborhood club they couldn't pay to get into, just because. Cuban society had created an environment in which Bangs's version of punk—the rebellion-for-rebellion's-sake kind, not my pop punk, Joe Strummer-as-progressive-prophet version—thrived. Liván and his crew were just the ones who applied the word to themselves.

For them, G Street fulfilled the same functions as the Internet: email, Facebook, and YouTube, rolled into one, a place for party planning and public identity shaping, a place to go to seek an audience for whatever you wanted to perform. I'd gone to a breakdancing practice session once and watched skinny kids spin and flip and shout and clap for one another in an abandoned restaurant with marble floors and full-length frames that had once held windows. At night, they performed on G.

G Street was also how trends spread. With only state-controlled media and no advertising campaigns to push products or fads through society, trends relied on subcultures and gossip. For example: A fashion-conscious skater watches a video of skating tricks on a friend's dad's PC and sees a trucker hat; looks cool, he thinks, and he finds some old fisherman on the *malecón* who's wearing one, a really old one. "Compadre," he says, "I'll give you 5 *kooks.*" He sews it back up or frays it a bit or maybe he gets a friend who's in graphic design school to draw a tag on it, make it look cooler. Other kids see him on G Street; what the hell is he wearing, they think—until they see the same style in a 2004 American movie that's showing on TV or in a dog-eared copy of, maybe, a *People* magazine or *TV y Notas* that some tourist left behind years ago. Aha, they think. They find hats, too.

G Street was alive in a way the Internet could never be. The *frikis* didn't have to talk to the *mikis* for their joint presence to say, *We are here, and there are so many of us.* They all refused, in their tiny, fashion-conscious ways, to accept the dreary reality of state stores that sold things they couldn't afford. And even Communist Party cars had to slow down around the intersection at Twenty-Third on Friday nights because the streets were so swollen with people. But G Street was vulnerable to its physicality, too.

First, its dimly lit spaces would diminish as high-powered floodlights were installed up and down the avenue. The gray-suited cops, young, burly men from the provinces who stood in sets of three or four with their hands deep in their pockets, multiplied. And one day, when I would hop up on a retaining wall to sit and wait for friends, I'd feel pointy rocks jab into my backside and stand up, an angry glow spreading through my chest. They'd been set in a fresh layer of concrete to discourage loitering. I thought of the *friki* who'd attended the first few punk rock shows sponsored by the Union of Young Communists back in 2007. Had the speaker wires been too new, the ambiance incongruously upbeat? I'd once heard a bouncy young emcee shout, "On the anti-imperialist stage, long live rock-and-roll!" and "Let's enjoy some good rock music!"

The police were nominally monitoring G Street to catch drug use, because what drugs were sold in Havana could be found on or around the avenue. But for the most part, the people who had the money to spend on illegal drugs, about five times more expensive per person than a $1 box of *Ron Planchao*, weren't really the sort who hung out on G Street. Those people were more elite than Liván and Takeshi; they could afford club entries and got their trends from black-market DVDs of new Hollywood releases and friends who traveled to Spain. Sure, some kids snorted ground-up, state-issued painkillers and bought Ketamine for 5 CUC each in the dank stairwells of nearby apartment buildings. But it was more common to overhear the two guys who told everyone that they were vegetarian vampires and lived off the human energy released by sex, trying to convince a girl that really, it was true, than to catch someone in the act of a drug deal. Not much of anything actually *happened* on G Street.

And that was the point. G Street was a place to be unique together, rebellious and risky enough to be a public register of boredom without actually placing young adults in much danger. In any case, it made them feel that they were doing something: being seen, being different, pissing someone off, getting away with it.

4

AMIGOS

SANDRA

*I was hanging around the restaurant Floridita, spending time
in the red light district, roulette in all the hotels, slot machines
spilling rivers of silver dollars, the Shanghai Theater, where for a
dollar twenty-five you could take in an extremely filthy stripshow,
and in the intermission see the most pornographic x-rated films
in the world. And suddenly it occurred to me that this extraordinary
city, where all vices were tolerated and all deals were possible,
was the real backdrop for my novel.*

—Graham Greene, on *Our Man in Havana*

If there was one thing Sandra knew well, it was hair. She knew hair
from root to split end. In beauty school, she had learned the
shape of the human head and how the best thing to do when
trimming its hair was to section the skull into eighths, she
told me the first time I met her. Her long nails shone red
as she held her hands in front of her to demonstrate on an
imaginary client. Her gold rings glinted. When she tired of

hair-cutting techniques, she waved her hands and her fingers sparked in the thick night like fireworks.

I'd shown up at the intersection of *malecón* and Paseo that night with Juan, who wanted to introduce me to Sandra. He'd shaken hands with a group of roving musicians in baseball hats encrusted with silver sequins and asked if anyone had seen la China, the nickname Sandra's slanted eyes had earned her. We'd sat down by the water and within ten minutes Sandra crossed the street toward us, taking deliberate, high steps; shaking her head to free her hair from ornate, dangly earrings; and looking at us with half-closed eyes as if we held a camera that shot photos for *Vogue*. Juan had introduced me, said I was doing book research and I'd explain the rest—and then he'd gone in search of cigarettes and disappeared. Sandra had flicked sharp eyes along my body, taking in my flats and bare face as I leaned against the waist-high seawall. She'd swung up next to me and I offered her the extra can of Cristal beer that I'd bought. When she spoke, her voice was throaty and low, and I thought more of New Jersey than Cuba.

Sandra, like some of the other girls who hung out where we sat on *malecón* where it hit Paseo, wore fashionable clothes of the barely there variety: diminutive shorts with interlocking C's on back pockets, sparkly heels, bras that peeked out from under tank tops, and halters that exposed midriffs. She dyed her own long, straight hair an inky blue-black and lined her lips with the same dark pencil that she used around her eyes because shops hadn't carried red in months. Her plastic nails were thick and whispery along the tips; she grabbed my forearm as we crossed the street on our way to the bathroom, dodging the cars that sped around the curve at Paseo. We went the long way to avoid the police who hung in the shadows on the intersection's traffic island, keeping an eye out for illicit activity on the strip. "The cars here, they'll hit you. And if it's him"—Sandra flicked her chin and pulled her hand down to mime a beard, the universal gesture for Fidel Castro—"they won't stop. They'll run you over and keep on going."

There were clubs and bars at the hotels that hulked over the crossroads—the mod Riviera, the shimmery Meliá Cohiba, the Jazz Café—but since few locals could afford drinks there, the tourists who wanted to meet Cubans hung out by the sea. Everyone, Cuban and foreign, loved the *malecón*, to sit facing the ocean and Miami and feel the spray on bare shins, or to turn toward the city and watch old cars roar by, or, after a long night at the bars, to see the edge of the sea begin to separate from a brightening sky. On nights when there was no moon, you could nod approvingly at the fish that men in mesh tank tops caught on almost-invisible lines that stretched from coils on the sidewalk. On hot days, you watched kids who leapt from the wall into high tide, cringing as their arms pinwheeled past the rocks cragging up from the ocean.

So young men toted bongo drums and guitars, imitating the Buena Vista Social Club for a few dollars' tip. Gentlemen in frayed straw fedoras asked tourists to pick up an extra beer at the gas station kiosk. Tired-looking women in Lycra shorts sang out the names of cones of roasted peanuts, *cucuruchos de maní*, and popcorn, *rositas de maíz*. Nonchalant girls cocked hips at the foreign men who walked past. Sandra had been taught the art of artifice to serve the Cuban Revolution through its beauty parlors, but she'd given up on hair. By the time she was twenty-one, she'd been working as a prostitute for around five years. The dates changed every time I asked her. Either way, she made about three times in one night what she'd have been paid monthly at any of the government-owned salons.

/// The statistics that Cuba's government likes to highlight when asked about the role of women in its Communist society are these: Before 1959, women had represented only 13 percent of the workforce and many were domestic servants. A large number were prostitutes, too—as a port city with a sexually liberal climate and a U.S.-backed puppet government, Havana was where *yanquis* had gone in search of louche, uninhibited nightlife from Prohibition on. The 1919 Volstead Act pushed Americans south and ballooned tourism numbers from thirty-three thousand visitors to Cuba in 1914 to fifty-six thousand in 1920 and ninety thousand in 1928. U.S. Navy boats, too, were usually docked in the bay. By 1931, seventy-four hundred women officially stated their professions as prostitutes and countless more didn't. The city formerly known as "the pearl of the Caribbean" was soon referred to as its brothel.

When the Revolution swept through, gambling and prostitution were outlawed. Castro had insisted that tourism could continue in Havana in the absence of its more morally questionable attractions—he'd welcomed more than two thousand people to a meeting of the American Society of Travel Agents in Havana in October 1959, ten months into his tenure. But soon enough, the missile crisis launched the Cold War, the U.S. trade and travel embargo was put in place, and American trips to Havana were curbed. Forty years after the 1959 Revolution, long after prostitutes had been trained as seamstresses and given jobs and day care for their children, 51 percent of Cuba's scientists were women. Fifty percent of attorneys and 52 percent of medical doctors, too. Everyone was paid nearly equally—a doctor, male or female, made marginally more than a seamstress, around $20 a month in Cuban pesos.

But then the Special Period happened, and the rations of food, clothing, and other necessities that removed pressure from those monthly stipends dwindled. Women—and some men—increasingly began to trade sexual favors for, say, the fish that a neighbor caught or the bread that only a well-placed state employee got very much of. When the government pushed to increase tourism and Cuba drew closer to the global capitalist marketplace, those activities again had cash value. By 1995, around the same time that studies on gender parity in the workforce came out, the Italian travel magazine *Viaggiare* had given the island the dubious honor of being the number one global "paradise of sexual tourism." The government, broke and desperate, did little to contradict this image. And though the economy lifted as Cuba rounded into the twenty-first century, and though the new decade saw police tossing the more obvious prostitutes into jail, sex was something that could be easily bought and sold in Havana.

And yet one key fact still sets Cuba apart: There aren't many pimps or third-party intermediaries in the sex trade. A police state with tightly restricted access to weapons and severe penalties for drugs creates an underworld more seamy than overtly violent. And few romantic liaisons between locals and foreigners are deemed prostitution. Rather, most fall under the banner of relationships with *amigos*. Any non-Cuban is eligible, and what locals want from *amigos* is neither finite nor clear, a mix of money, attention, and the sense of possibility linked to anyone with a non-Cuban passport. Some of these men get their women out of the country. More frequently, they are maintained for a while before being dropped when the men find newer, younger girls or grow tired of Cuba, its heat, and its drama.

In the way that the language of a city fills in the blanks of what its people want to name, sometime between the early nineties and today the word *jinetero/a* became the catch-all to describe Cuba's hookers and hustlers, people who seek foreign currency or CUC, the valuable tourist cash, rather than the pesos in which government salaries are paid, via foreigners. The word's provenance isn't clear. *Jinete* in Spanish is a horse jockey; whether this means that women hold the reins of the "horses" is unclear. Today, the masculine *jinetero* refers insultingly to a man who caters to tourists in any questionably legal, hustler-like capacity. *Jinetera* means "a Cuban woman who trades sex for money."

I had avoided *jineteros* and *jineteras* since I'd first come to Cuba. But I couldn't write about women in Havana without talking to a *jinetera*, said Juan, whom I'd met the year before and who loved documenting his city's underbelly, and I agreed.

"You may have to pay her," he told me the day after he'd introduced me to Sandra. I sat with him and his girlfriend, Alejandra, on the terrace of the maze-like Vedado house they shared with Juan's mother, stepfather, and three other families, talking about *jineteras*. Their baby daughter slept in Juan's lap and Alejandra's son from a previous relationship drew at the kitchen table.

I cringed, and he shrugged.

"I mean, you are using time of hers in which she'd potentially be paid by someone else if you weren't there."

"Especially when you see her at night," said Alejandra.

"She seemed fine with just talking to me," I said. "I won't pay her for her time, but I guess I can buy her pizza, beers, pay for taxis, and hope that's enough."

Juan looked skeptical, but Alejandra nodded. "That'll probably work. After all, you're foreign," she said, cocking her head as she looked at me. I felt suddenly uncomfortable. "There's opportunity, of a sort, associated with just your presence."

/// Sometimes it's hard to discern who's selling sex and who's just trying to wear as little fabric as possible in

Havana's oppressive heat. The mainstays of *jinetera* fashion— miniskirts, transparent fabrics, cleavage- and shoulder-baring tops—appear on most women, including foreigners, who feel freer to be sexy in permissive Cuba than at home. At clubs, I saw foreign women with bikini strap marks sunburned around their necks look left and right and then pull their necklines down before dancing with slim Cuban men in tight jeans and big belt buckles. These women lapped up the sensual aura by the minute, as if just breathing would send tiny cells of sexy through their bodies, the infusion pushing and pulling hips back and forth, transforming walks into sashays, planting dry one-liners in mouths.

Sandra had long since mastered these feminine tricks. Everything about her physical appearance was calibrated to entice: the tops that looked almost about to show too much skin, the hair that twisted around her neck, her long, soft, red nails. I had just five years on Sandra, but I felt large, clumsy, and dusty around her in my flats and loose dresses. I was a tattered stuffed animal next to her Barbie doll as we sat, the second time we met, in the back seat of a state-owned cab that took us from the *malecón* out to her house.

Sandra had recently moved from La Corea, one of Havana's few slum-like neighborhoods, into a nicer but smaller dwelling in San Miguel del Padrón. Her home was in a six-by-eight-block patch between a fetid stream and the main road that linked downtown Havana with the outer boroughs like San Francisco de Paula, where Ernest Hemingway lived. San Miguel was a place of contrasts: A street began with a few freshly painted houses near the road to San Francisco and faded into cinderblock shacks with stretched-out oil barrels for fences closer to the stream. Egg cartons, plastic bags, the rusted skeletons of metal chairs, and fruit rinds bobbed in the water.

The shiny taxi slowed as we pulled onto her street, dodging potholes. A couple on the corner stared at us and Sandra waved. A few feet away, an old man in overalls, a burlap sack of oranges slung over his right shoulder, stood at attention and saluted. Sandra dissolved into giggles, slapping the vinyl seat. "What a *loco, loco loquito*," she gasped. "¿Viste?" She jumped out as soon as we pulled up on her block and leaned against the car's trunk, picking at her nails as I paid the fare.

Years ago, Sandra's mother had kicked her out of the house. She now lived with her grandmother, Aboo, and her half-brother, Gallego, in a two-room apartment in what had once been a yard at the center of a block, down an alley and behind a single-story home with neoclassical columns and a street-side patio. Aboo didn't approve of Sandra staying out for days on end, but Sandra's father was in Florida and her mother had a new husband, a nice house in suburban La Lisa, and a set of twin toddlers. And the money Sandra brought home supported their household.

For every woman supported by foreign men, I'd heard it estimated that three more Cuban citizens got by on the money, whether directly or not. Sandra, Aboo, and Gallego, at least. The government didn't do much aside from tossing a too-blatant hooker into Villa Delicia, the nickname for the women's jail. Sandra had spent four days there when she was nineteen and had eaten so little she'd come out "this thin," she told me, holding up her pinkie. If men stopped coming to the island, tempted no longer by images of scantily clad *mulattas* on white sand beaches and bodies pressed together in crowded bars, hotel rooms would languish unvisited, and taxis would have fewer fares and restaurants more empty tables. The area's policemen, Sandra said, were eminently bribable, for the right price.

Just inside Sandra's door, a small table and two matching chairs were piled high with folded clothes. The room also held a wooden armoire, a stereo, and a refrigerator near a small kitchenette. A photo of a man with a guitar named Juan Manuel, signed to *China la más bella*, hung on the wall beside images of Sandra in a tiered pink dress for her *quinceañera* and a collage of family and friends, the toddlers in La Lisa, and the neighborhood girls. The back room held two twin beds and a closet. Sandra poked around for a box of photos. When she found it, we returned to the central patio, where two more of the table set's chairs gathered rust at the joints, to sit under the laundry lines that the three families who lived in the middle of the block used on alternating days. She set the box on the ground and sorted through pictures. I pulled out a pack of cheap, unfiltered Criollo cigarettes, which I favored for their clean tobacco and sweet aftertaste. Sandra wrinkled her nose but took one anyway, and used it to point out the Spanish guy who'd asked her to marry him two years ago. He'd walked in on her a few weeks later with someone else. She still had the ring.

Sandra had sex for the first time when she was eleven (the average age in Cuba is around thirteen) with a man whose name she'd tattooed across the small of her back, *Mumúa*, above an image of two doves entwined with scrolls. He was thirty-two then, and even now he was "crazy for me," she said as she lit another cigarette, though he was in jail for selling stolen motorcycle parts. What had begun as nights out slid quickly into prostitution—government salaries paled next to the $50 that Sandra could make for a night with a man, nearly always foreign, nearly always Spanish, Cuban American, or Italian. So she quit, never finished her certificate course at beauty school.

The gate at the street end of the alley jingled as Gallego walked in and, after introductions, I picked up my bag to leave. Sandra asked me where I was going. "To meet some friends downtown," I said. There weren't many decent restaurants in Havana then and a generous and growing cast of acquaintances and friends, Cubans and a few expatriates, regularly invited me around to eat. She gave me a once-over and pushed me toward the floor-length mirror in her living room. If I'd just do my hair *like this*, she told me as she reached into my curls and flipped them into a messy, voluminous updo, I'd look way sexier. A red wash to make the dull brown more interesting would do me good. And my shorts could be shorter, too. I should also line my lips. You know, show off contours. I handed her bobby pins for my hair but liked my shorts the way they were, mid-thigh. She looked skeptical, the pins between her lips as she styled and then hands on her hips once she'd finished. It did look better.

The next time I saw Sandra was a quick visit on the *malecón* again. Just before I left, she told me she'd come up with a plan: When I went back to Mexico, I should get my company to write her a *carta de invitación*. "They can say I'll be working for them," she said. "What kind of company do you work at? A newspaper or something, right? They wouldn't even have to offer me a job, just do the *carta*; I can take care of myself once I get there. And then I'll just stay."

I didn't really work for anyone, at least not like that, I explained, and some of the magazines I wrote for were actually based in Europe. She looked at me coyly. "Whatever," she said. I paused and then smiled a little and said that I could hardly get them to do favors for me, much less for an amiga in Cuba. Sandra shrugged and began to gossip about a neighbor of hers that I'd met the day I'd visited her house. She'd come to borrow Sandra's fake plastic spectacles because the amigo who was here for a week liked "the smart look"—funny, right?

There was no change in her demeanor, as if the desire to go to Mexico had left her as soon as her shoulders had moved.

/// The big turquoise hotel where Sandra hung out, the Habana Riviera, was originally commissioned by gangster Meyer Lansky's front men to be his mob's Havana gambling hub, an extravagant high-rise with sophistication unrivaled in the Caribbean—Manhattan on the Florida Straits. Architect Philip Johnson did initial designs until he realized he'd be working for the mafia and passed on the job. The building opened in December 1957 with Ginger Rogers and her musical revue in the hotel's Copa Cabaret and immediately became a destination for the American jet set and the Cubans they favored. But in the end, Lansky's henchmen and Hollywood hangers-on enjoyed only three years of the broad views of ocean and skyline from the 352 rooms before Castro nationalized the hotel and casino in 1960.

Today, the walls of many of the Riviera's rooms buckle from unaddressed humidity. Only half of them have seen the necessary renovations after fifty years of use; most floors are only partly habitable and some are closed altogether. Viewed from the huge saltwater pool, to which $10 buys anyone a day pass, the broken curtain rods dangling diagonally across half of the windows above give the hotel the look of a cross-eyed old man. What beds there are have been made up with linens in sizes that don't fit the mattresses, and cockroaches skitter around the hallways or lie belly-up in corners. But in the lobby, the imagination sketches outlines of the three-piece suits and stiff silk skirts of the past, ghost-like, conjured by the décor. Low-slung, coral velvet couches and surfboard-shaped coffee tables with opalescent mosaic and gold inlay, all well-preserved, invite a time-travel fantasy. The broad leaves of tropical trees in planters loll over gleaming furniture and magenta rugs, and the north-facing windows look directly over the *malecón* and out to the sea.

Lobbies were places where one could forget the hotels and houses that were crumbling for lack of maintenance, ignore the damp bubbles at the corners of the walls. But hotels and other tourist haunts—restaurants, cabarets—were where the *jineteras* stood out for their incongruity with their surroundings. They sat in red lace tops in the plush pink cushions of rattan loungers at the Hotel Nacional, drinking mojitos and studying the menu as amigos checked email on smartphones; they ate in pairs at the in-home restaurants, ordering rice and beans and plantain tostones while the men across the candles scarfed down chicken; and, in the car rental agency, they did the talking while the men stood back and studied the map of Cuba on the wall with a different cartoon for each state.

Lobbies were also places where hotel security could most easily identify the women in spandex and pleather halter tops. The Riviera was Sandra's beat. Some nights she'd stay out on the *malecón* and other nights she'd slip one of the hotel workers 5 or 10 CUC to stay from around nine at night until she found a client. The $50 she charged gave her a good profit margin. She'd order a TuKola at the bar and proposition any man whose eyes lingered on her, murmuring words like "girl" and "the night." At the club, now called the Copa Room, she'd shimmy up against a man and make him feel like he was the best dancer in the room. She complained later about their terrible dance moves and sometimes she stopped walking in the middle of a San Miguel street, raised her arms straight out to either side, and shuffled awkwardly back and forth while shivering with giggles to show me how badly they moved, but someone usually took her up to his room or whisked her off in a taxi to another hotel.

A tenuous confidence built between Sandra and me. I'd sit with Sandra on her patio and watch the nightly Brazilian telenovela on her neighbor's TV, which he dragged to the shared patio outside. Her neighbor was leaving for Panama soon, where he'd work as a physical therapist, always any day now. I watched her untangle her ten-year-old neighbor's jumping rope and tally scores from the lotería, the numbers racket that all of San Miguel played, on small scraps of chicken-scratched paper, and, though she diligently tried to explain how numbers were assigned to lucky objects and happenings, I never understood the rules. Other days, we'd drink cheap coffees or beers in the cafés in San Miguel and talk about not very much and then we'd hitchhike downtown together, where I'd leave her around the Riviera and head back home. I wore Birkenstocks to Sandra's spike heels and demurred when she asked me to buy her a cell phone or told me how great her half-brother was in bed.

One afternoon I met Sandra in a park in Habana Vieja and, when she started dropping hints about being hungry, we went for pizza at one of the area's many tourist-trap restaurants. Oil-stained white tablecloths hung limply atop vibrant red ones. We sat and, while I went to the bathroom, she flagged down the waiter and ordered a plate of olives.

"Ay, Julia," she sighed when I returned, stretching out the round vowels of my name, "estoy en estado." She shoveled the bland green olives into her mouth, filling her cheeks with them. She'd been eating like a horse, she said, peeing four times an hour, and had what looked like a spare tire—she thought it was Mumúa's baby. He'd gotten out of jail recently and was the only man with whom she didn't use a condom.

Abortions were free and relatively fast and she'd terminated pregnancies in the past, but they'd told her that any more would endanger her ability to ever have kids, so she would have a child in seven months. "Besides, I'm alone," she said quickly as if brushing the obvious fact from her shoulder.

"It's not the same to have someone to live for, someone to fight for, as it is to be alone. Aboo will die, my mother doesn't talk to me, and Gallego runs off with anything with a skirt. I need someone."

Mumúa wanted to make a family of them, but Sandra had a plan, she reported, jaunty again as she dipped French fries in the olive brine. She'd tell Bong, the Italian who visited Havana every four months with a millionaire invalid boss, that he was the father. As Sandra told it, theirs was a torrid, Jane-Austen-in-the-tropics tale, the hunt for an advantageous match. Bong, who had a wife and kid back in Italy, wanted to move to Cuba to be with her, but his boss, who had promised to leave his fortune to Bong, wouldn't hear of it, so they snuck around. Since he was crazy about Sandra, and he looked something like Mumúa, she'd tell him the baby was his. Then he'd support her until the old man died and Bong could divorce the wife, marry Sandra, and take her and "their" baby away from Cuba, or at least to a better house on the island. "If he asks for a genetic test, I'll just say no," she summed up, bobbing her head between bites of food.

The details were fuzzy, though. She had never actually seen the invalid boss. In one version of the story, Bong hailed from a town in Italy where everyone looked like they were Asian—Sandra wasn't sure which town, didn't care—and in another he was actually Filipino Italian.

When I asked her what she'd do for money if she did leave, she was dismissive: "Aiouuuuuulia, anything, anything," she said with a wave of her hand. She was a young, single mother with a ninth-grade education and few marketable skills. In Cuba, her baby would be guaranteed health care in a system that boasted a laudable record; despite the decrepit appearances of most of the country's hospitals, world health organizations cite Cuba's infant mortality rate as better than that of the United States. Her child would learn to read and Sandra would be guaranteed at least some food to get him or her through the first few years.

Sandra's plans for the future were like clouds she thought she'd walk into; they'd envelop her and then everything would be different. She'd find a boyfriend who'd marry her and get her the hell out of Cuba, where the life she'd lived for twenty-one years bored her: the same inadequate ration food, the same lack of privacy, the same eternal wait for buses to get downtown, the gloom that rolled in when her days were occupied by sleeping and boredom. It was the languid sense of time—which I soaked up in Havana—that suffocated Sandra. Foreigners opened up wormholes of opportunity: Sandra could have money, sleep in hotels, buy H. Upmann cigarettes for $1, eat her favorite dessert, Jell-O, every day. The dreams Sandra imagined were the size of all the rooms she'd ever been in.

A few weeks after we'd had dinner, Sandra stopped talking to Mumúa. She'd seen him zipping toward home on his motorcycle with a pretty little thing clinging to his back. Privately, I was glad that Mumúa was out of Sandra's life. So she'd listed Gallego as the baby's father on her *carnet de embarazada*, the I.D. card with which a pregnant woman can claim state benefits. With her *carnet*, she was entitled to medical care throughout her pregnancy, including house calls if she couldn't make it to the clinic and enough sonogram pictures to show off to neighbors, plus, she said, "a cradle that never shows up, a roll of gauze to use as diapers, little bottles of perfume and cream, two baby outfits, and four cloth diapers." She had already bought an extra roll of gauze from a woman who would use disposables. In stores, disposables retailed for around $12 for a pack of twenty, or, on the black market, $14 for forty. Sandra hoped that, if Bong pulled through and decided to support "his" child, she'd use disposables once the baby came. It wasn't an exit visa, but it was progress.

/// "If you could just get her to dress differently from the rest of the *jineteras*, maybe wear less skimpy clothes, you know, less spandex, she'd make more money," Lucía said at lunch one afternoon.

I'd told her what Sandra had also said to me that spring: that she'd been having a hard time finding clients even before she'd gotten pregnant. Lucía was taking English classes at the TV station so she'd be better prepared to leave once she got her exit visa. The process had stalled: It would be something like two years, long enough that she just waved her hand into the muddled future in explanation, before she could get an appointment with the Spaniards. And her family friends in Chile had visited Santiago—they lived a few hours from the capital—without getting an email from her confirming that she did in fact need them to file her *carta de invitación.* They'd come and gone from the city and wouldn't be back for another two months. Another two months before the paperwork would be filed. The news had launched Lucía into a week of puffy eyes.

In any case, we spent an afternoon every week or two trying to talk in English and usually failing. We often wound up watching *Friends* with English subtitles instead. Lucía wrote down the words she didn't know and paused the show every few minutes to ask me the vocabulary she'd missed and then laugh at the jokes she hadn't gotten. Our conversation had begun in English but we'd flipped back into Spanish because she didn't know how to say "prostitute" or "dress."

"Well, but she'd never listen to me. She thinks I'm a lost cause, I think. Or asexual, or gay, or something," I told her. "But not someone to consult on how to get men."

Neither was Lucía, to be honest. The one time she knew clearly that she'd found love, she had told me—not flirtation, not boredom, not a challenge—her love had up and moved to Miami. Lucía got knocks at the door sometimes on Valentine's Day, men who held money sent from Florida via the underground version of Western Union, and otherwise she kept it casual in the realm of love. Flings who left the morning after, even when they were repeat visitors, or who acted like friends.

That day Lucía had made a rich pinto bean stew over rice with slices of salted avocado. "But the *jineteras* who leave just a little bit to the imagination get the richer tourists," she said. Her mouth twisted with a combination of sympathy and cynicism, the sense that she was in on something that Sandra wouldn't intuit. This was reflexive knowledge for Alejandra and Elaine, too, who often asked after Sandra. They and Lucía had known women who sold sex, but the high-school-or-college-educated sort, who worked casually and only sometimes and wore clothes that were either tight or revealing but not often both. "Obviously."

/// Tourism statistics in Cuba didn't dip in 2009, after the U.S. recession and Hurricane Ike, but Sandra swore there were fewer foreigners around. And since she was visibly pregnant during more or less the same period, she had moved on to a second money-making plan. She and Yessica bought two hundred cups of yogurt every few days of the sort that retailed in the *kook* supermarkets for 75 cents each. They paid a middleman 15 cents per cup and then walked the neighborhood to sell the yogurts door to door at three for a dollar, doubling their profits.

Anyone who had seen Sandra and Yessica pushing their yogurt-filled baby stroller down the streets of San Miguel might have wondered at what would have been a very pudgy child inside it. I had shown up at Sandra's place, but Aboo had told me that they were wandering. I found them near the main avenue, struggling to free the stroller from one of the holes that yawned across the street. Yessica and I took charge of the stroller, while Sandra waddled along the sidewalk, sticking her head into open doorways and windows to tell people that she was selling yogurts for half the store price. Every few doors, someone would come out, hand them a few *kooks*, lift the yellow, lacy blanket that covered the stroller's seat, and paw through its contents for the desired flavors.

Sandra was imminently due. Her stretchy pink and gray T-shirt snuck up her belly, which protruded nearly a foot from her petite frame, revealing thick purplish marks. When I'd come and gone from Havana at some point earlier in her pregnancy, Sandra had exhorted me to bring her cream for her stretch marks. "What do I have if not this body I've got," she'd said, outlining her hips. "If I lose this body, I lose everything." When I returned, I brought cream and prenatal vitamins. "*Coño*," she had said, "gracias. I'll have to run these by my doctor, but I bet they'll really help."

We snaked through the area. "Baby's still cooking, China?" whistled the man who leaned against the counter of the near-bare corner bodega, where rations were dispensed. Sandra rolled her slightly slanted eyes.

"Child's coming out walking if she stays in much longer," muttered one woman as she sauntered by.

"When are you due?" asked a girl as she pressed her hands against Sandra's swollen belly. "Today? Tomorrow?"

"If it were up to me," she said, "I'd go straight to the hospital right now and get this baby the hell out of me." The temperature stretched toward a hundred degrees of mostly humidity.

When we reached the main avenue, Yessica and I stayed

on the sidewalk with the stroller as Sandra popped into shops—laundromat, cafeteria, Banco Nacional de Cuba—to advertise her wares. At the bank, the girls stopped for thirty minutes to rest in the air-conditioned ATM cabin, which hardly anyone used, and sort out who wanted what inside. They ferried pineapple and strawberry yogurts to customers and sold upward of forty cups while I stayed with the stroller. If a policeman came, Yessica said sternly, I was to invent some excuse and ditch it. Sandra giggled: "The yuma comes to Cuba to sell yogurt. That's how bad the economy up north is." When one yogurt spilled open and the bitter smell of synthetic strawberry began to stink, Sandra whisked a towel embroidered with a yellow duckie out of her purse, which had at one point been my purse, a black faux–patent leather tote I'd given her—she'd noted at our Habana Vieja pizza dinner what a good diaper bag it would make, and I'd left it with her. She wiped up the yogurt and stuffed the damp towel into the interior zip compartment.

Once the stroller was empty, Yessica turned it back toward home and Sandra walked me toward the bus stop. It was late afternoon and the amber air was dusty. As we paused at a corner to let a truck turn, she pivoted toward me. "I'd like to ask you something," she said. "Will you be the baby's godmother?"

I felt her at my side, gauging my response as she studied the ends of her long hair for split ends. The truck passed and we crossed the street. I needed to redraw the lines between us, I knew then, and if that meant she'd toss me aside, foreign and writer and all, I'd do it anyway. I wished that there was a part of me that wanted to say yes, or believe she'd asked me out of genuine sentiment, but there wasn't. The problem, I explained to Sandra, was that though a friendship had developed between us, I was still interviewing her in a professional capacity. If I was the godmother of her child, I would be seen as being too involved, and my "bosses," hazy as they were, would find even our formal interviews suspect. She nodded. We were on the main street among sweaty men in undershirt tanks, old ladies with shopping bags, and girls with hair in netted ballerina buns. We passed under shaded colonnades that had been painted, vandalized, and repainted darker shades, a mottled patchwork of scratched-out signatures, expletives encased in bubbles, and declarations of love, "PR+SN" and "Yosey Lulu."

Sandra shook her head and pursed her lips. "No," she said. She laughed and, after a beat, nodded. "Of course I'd rather maybe be famous. You just keep doing your job. Yessica wanted to be godmother anyway."

/// Two days later, Mia Jacqueline was born. In Sandra's freezer, which was only slightly cooler than the tepid main compartment of her refrigerator, yogurts were still stacked three-deep. On her first day home, the day after Mia's birth, five neighborhood children were playing in front of Sandra's house. A nearby gingko tree had been shorn and its limbs, studded with bunches of large, hard green seeds, were strewn throughout the street. The kids collected the seeds, which resembled neon olives peeking through the cages made by their cupped hands. High-pitched squeals carried across the street as the children taunted whoever's collection quota was slipping behind the average. Soon they'd accumulated two Lilliputian mountains in the pots they'd spirited from their mothers' kitchens. They planned to tell everyone that they were grapes, which was the most expensive item for sale in the fruit market, and sell them by the bucket.

A skinny horse pulled a man down the street on a carriage made of splintery planks of wood. The man banged a hammer against a thin strip of aluminum, collecting organic trash and grass to feed to the horse. I sat on a stoop with one of Sandra's neighbors, whose boyfriend had gone to the hospital to give Sandra a ride home in his small Russian car. The neighbor and I smoked cigarettes and talked about her kids.

As the car pulled up, with Gallego cradling the tiny, sleeping baby in his arms, the kids crowded around it, leaving finger-shaped smears on the windows. They hooted until the street's mothers emerged and shouted them home, saying they'd have to visit later. Sandra and Gallego emerged from the car looking every bit the part of exhausted new parents.

Sandra hobbled down the alley toward her apartment, bleary-eyed. Everything hurt, she said. Everything. All non-essential furniture in her two rooms had been moved outside to the patio that she shared with two other families. A crib had been assembled in the windowless back bedroom, and the two twin mattresses that Aboo, Gallego, and Sandra shared in turns were piled one atop another to make room for it. Her father in Florida had sent a suitcase of baby goods and Sandra would sell the overstock. Fourteen baby bottles decorated with Winnie the Pooh licking honey from a jar sat atop the old washing machine that was the kitchen counter between cleaning days.

I sat in a rocking chair next to Sandra. The baby squirmed on her knees. She had stuffed her bra full of tissue paper and stowed a lighter between her swollen breasts, and she waved to gesture that I should light a cigarette for her. I grabbed the packet off the table, lit the cigarette, and handed it to her; she kept one hand on the baby's belly and held the cigarette with the other.

The Cuban government almost never granted exit papers for children. The consequences of this fact hadn't seemed real, I supposed, until Sandra had held Mia. This would be her life, she spat—these two rooms, these neighbors, motherhood. My presence in her home felt suddenly cruel. I sipped my coffee, nodded, and slipped away after fifteen minutes or so.

/// It was a few weeks before I went out to San Miguel again. White baby linens hung thick as curtains on the patio's laundry lines. Aboo waved me inside, brushing off my offers to help her hang the white gauze squares they had cut to use as diapers. Sandra was out, the baby was asleep in her crib, and I sat down to wait. I'd brought a bag of old clothes, girly hand-me-downs from Juan and Alejandra's toddler that they'd in turn been given by friends and neighbors. An army of ants carried thumbnail-sized bread crumbs up the lavender wall. The room smelled tangy. When Sandra arrived half an hour later, she bustled into the apartment, pulled open her black faux-patent purse, and asked me if I wanted to buy some air fresheners. I laughed, relieved that she seemed happier.

"So that's what you're doing for money now," I said.

She shook her head and busied herself making coffee. "Nah, not for long. An *amigo* comes out this weekend from Spain—he's Cuban but he lives in Spain—and I ran into his daughter around here last week. 'China, he's crazy to see you,' she says, and I tell her that I've just given birth, so she comes to see the baby. Of course she said Mia was beautiful. She is a cute baby, thank god. Anyway, 'You call me as soon as the *cuarentena* is done,' the girl says; 'you can see my dad as soon as you're ready.'" So, she continued, she was cutting short her *cuarentena*, the forty days in which mothers were admonished by Cuban nurses not to engage in sexual activity with new partners.

Mia woke up with a yowl and Sandra asked me to grab her while she prepared a bottle. She was trying to stop breast-feeding so her breasts wouldn't sag too much, she said, so she was giving the baby formula that her father had sent out from Miami. I watched her, ten feet away from me in her kitchenette. The silence was swollen and barbed. I looked down at Mia: She had huge, chubby cheeks, and milky-blue, slightly slanted eyes, like Sandra's, but *shh*, she said—it was what made her look like Bong. I commented on how much she'd grown.

"Any news from Bong?" I asked.

"Well, he called the other day," she said, "first time I'd spoken to him since I told him I was having his baby, months ago, that time when the call dropped. 'Sandra,' he says, 'how's the baby?' Identical to you, I say. She's your carbon copy. 'Really,' he says. 'I can't wait to meet her.' Then the call went dead. He said he was coming next month, though."

Before I retreated to the illusory romance of downtown Havana, Sandra looked at me wide-eyed and asked me to do her an enormous favor. Could I lend her $5? To pay off the man who'd sold her the black-market yogurt once and for all? She promised she'd pay me back as soon as she could.

5

LIKE THE STARS

ISNAEL

Every day, Isnael arrived for work in the uniform of a *repartero*: faux Puma tennis shoes held together with tape, embellished Ed Hardy–style T-shirt, tight-ish jeans, and a belt with a silver Playboy bunny buckle. He'd turned twenty-one that year, but Isnael still had the limbs of a teenager. Every day, he changed into painting shorts and cheap sandals and worked with the expansive calm of a yogi, scrubbing old paint off the walls at the house of an expatriate acquaintance of mine for a few under-the-table dollars a day.

Katherine, the only American I knew in Havana, had recently moved in and hired a team of young men to help resuscitate her ramshackle Vedado house. The old woman from whom Katherine and her Cuban husband had bought the house—a former servant who'd been left behind in 1960 as guard until the Communists were gone and her employers could return from Miami—had rented it out to local film crews who made *telenovelas* in the living rooms. She'd had no source of income and though the Instituto Cubano de Artes Cinematográficas paid in pesos, they paid. A set designer had once used a cheap blue watercolor on the walls, which had faded almost instantaneously yet still clung persistently; repainting was futile and would only infect whatever color was laid atop the blue. Isnael's job was to use bucket after bucket of water to dilute the paint until it slid in slim rivulets over the ornate molding and into aquamarine puddles on the floor tiles. So he worked painstakingly in sections, beginning his mornings atop scaffolding at the height of the eighteen-foot ceilings and descending through the day.

The paint was capricious, Isnael told me the first time we met. "In places it comes off easy," he said as he pointed, with just a swipe of the rag he kept tucked in the belt loops of his cut-off jean shorts. In other spots, it wouldn't let go no matter how he scrubbed. He gestured to a crackled section near the molding. Even after he went over those areas with a toothbrush, the paint left sea-blue veins in the fissures of the old walls.

Isnael worked without complaints or questions, his three-inch afro and lanky brown arms freckled by the day's end. During his lunch breaks, he taught Katherine's son how to make an omelet or cheese sandwich. He often gave half of his lunch to the neighborhood strays. He looked constantly amused. After the departure of the other $3-a-day handymen, burly sweaty young men who hooted incessant jokes, Isnael stayed—he had become indispensable as babysitter, bartender, and all-around errand boy at the big old house.

He had gone to school to be a children's art teacher, I learned. There was such a shortage of teachers in Havana that a few years earlier the government had created a special high school curriculum to track teenagers directly into teaching jobs at age nineteen. But the pay wasn't as high as he'd been told it'd be, so after a few months he began to buy bread at the local bakery and wander into his neighborhood selling door-to-door at a slight markup. He quit teaching slowly, by not showing up except to collect the paychecks that came for three months after he taught his last class. Then he painted meticulous portraits of faces made of fruits and vegetables, banana noses and grapes for curly hair à la Giuseppe Arcimboldo, to sell black-market to an artist who claimed them as his at the tourist artisan fair. It was the painting middleman who'd passed on word of the wall-scrubbing gig.

If Isnael had a knack for patient work, work that required stillness and focus, he explained to me one day, it was because he was destined for it. He was a "son" of Yemayá, the *orisha* or goddess of the oceans and patron of motherhood. Her "children," divined in the third stage of initiation into Santería, were maternal, dignified, and nurturing. As he told me about his religion—"the religion," as it was called, to which 70 percent of Cubans reportedly adhered—he looked at me more intently. He gave such detailed answers to my questions about rituals, deities, and symbols that I swam in their specificity. His enthusiasm assumed everyone else's knowledge, too. It allowed no room for overview or backing up to the beginning. Neither his clothes nor his employment mattered as much to him as this, his religion.

Isnael felt spirits. That was how he first realized he had a gift, a calling, and that it was Santería: he would dream something, and then, days, weeks, months later, it would occur. The spirits told him things. Disembodied voices sent him bits of knowledge, like this: One time Isnael was waiting for a bus, and he said to the friend he was with, "As soon as it's our turn to get on the bus, it's going to start raining." And it did. He never felt alone.

Maybe the spirits were why I kept coming back to his

country, I said to him idly one day. "Maybe someone here put a hex on me and I can't shake free of it." I laughed.

Isnael nodded. "We should find out," he said, gravely.

Havana had always felt suffused with a light mysticism, with coincidence and potential—my Communist Party god-father, people who connected me with the sources I sought, a home with Elaine and Nicolas. This was part of what had kept the city alive in my mind even when I was away for long stretches of time. I'd never been religious, but I'd also often found religion appealing in an arms-length, abstract way.

I was only mostly joking, I realized as I walked away.

/// Santería derives from the Yoruba tradition of West Africa; it first came to Cuba with the slaves that Spanish colonizers shipped out from current-day Nigeria and Benin to cut sugar-cane. Its rituals were cloaked in Catholicism during the years of iron-fisted, work-to-the-death colonial rule. Slaves wor-shipped icons of saints instead of their own *orishas*, Santería's pantheon of deities; *how devout*, the Spanish plantation own-ers might have thought, not knowing that Our Lady of Regla represented Yemayá and Saint Barbara stood in for Changó. Throughout the first half of the twentieth century, Santería proliferated mostly among black Cubans while white Cubans attended Catholic churches, even if only occasionally.

Fidel Castro's Revolution was at its start a white, middle-class one. His was a language of equality and indignation, but the men and women who fought with him were predomi-nantly white, so white that during the first battles with Batis-ta's army, the government men were shocked: "When Captain Yañes came upon Castro hiding asleep in a *bohío*, it will be recalled that the soldier who found them cried: *'Son blancos!'* They are white!. . . It is not clear how many of the rebel army in the Sierra were black but a majority certainly were not, and

Almeida, a mulatto, was the only officer of importance who was," wrote Hugh Thomas in his encyclopedic history *Cuba, or, the Pursuit of Freedom*. Cuba had long been a place where multiracial alliances coexisted with persistent racism and discrimination, a place where white families hired black help in order to emulate the American South but the president was a mulatto who may have had some Chinese and Indian blood, too. By the standards of demography, Batista was the more progressive leader. He was also a *santero*. Castro had gone to Catholic school.

But then the rebels claimed the country, and tens of thousands of the wealthiest whites fled to Florida, and Castro told American journalists in January 1959 that his new government would work to erase racial discrimination once and for all. That same month, Castro gave his first nationally televised speech. As he spoke, two white doves—the representation in Santería of Obatalá, the divinity who shapes humans from clay in heaven—flew in to perch on his shoulder and podium and rested there for the entire two hours of his half-marathon oration, their white wings tucked in at their sides. In 1962, a North American survey found that 80 percent of black Cubans were wholly in favor of the Revolution, compared to 67 percent of whites.

That decade, religion, with its hierarchies and costly rituals, was pushed out in the name of a higher order, that of Marx and Lenin. Socialist "new men" could not bow to an esoteric power. Religion was outlawed—Christmas was illegal—and Santería was again practiced covertly. But the religion's emphasis on quiet but tightly knit social structures lent organization to neighborhood communities. It was also promiscuously, exuberantly able to fold traits from other faiths into its rituals. Rituals from European spiritism and African *palo monte*, Catholic icons and chants popped up in

Santería ceremonies that likely seemed more practical, more visceral than baroque church rites. Where it had been known as the religion of the black maids before, Santería's following became more mixed as the racial, socioeconomic hierarchy of Cubans flattened, as universities got darker and Afro-Cuban rhythms pervaded airwaves and mixed-race marriages, like that of Isnael's parents, proliferated.

Then the U.S.S.R. fell. Socioeconomic equality among people with different skin tones backslid as remittances from Cuban Americans—who are, according to U.S. census information, 85 percent white, a bit more than 10 percent black or mixed-race—benefitted predominantly white Cubans. As the government pushed to attract tourists, it employed more whites than blacks, from taxi drivers to waiters to tour guides, in order to reflect the best possible vision of itself to visitors from arguably more racist European and Latin American nations. Flicking on the TV to watch a Cuban *telenovela* revealed whites in leading roles. Papers like "Are Blacks 'Getting Out of Control?' Racial Attitudes, Revolution, and Political Transition in Cuba," which stole part of its title from a white Havanan's response to a 1994 riot in a blacker neighborhood, were published in sociology journals in the United States.

Estimates of Cuba's racial breakdown vary wildly. On the government's 2002 country-wide census, black and mixed-race Cubans were reported to compose 35 percent of the country's population. The U.S. State Department and the University of Miami's Institute for Cuban and Cuban-American Studies puts the figure at 62 percent. Cuban economist and political scientist Esteban Morales Domínguez, whose 2007 book *The Challenges of the Racial Problem in Cuba* was published in Havana by one of the main local academic presses, raised that number to somewhere between 62 and 72 percent, because mixed-race Cubans, he said, claimed their white heritage on the self-reported census. What's most likely is that about a third of the country is of pure European descent, or white; another third is of African descent, or black; and a final third is something in between, or mulatto, the decidedly un-PC term that Cubans use, often tenderly in conversation and defiantly in official documents.

In 2005, Morales Domínguez found, 73 percent of scientists and technicians were white. Eighty percent of professors at the University of Havana, too, and these numbers held for the rest of the country. Blacks were unemployed at double the rate of whites, which, he wrote, led to more black-market activities, and therefore jails filled with 85 percent darker-skinned Cubans. Anecdotally, this would explain why blacks were stopped by police on streets at far higher rates than whites. But that was more likely due to the fact that an overwhelming majority of Cubans—three-quarters—agreed with the statement that "racial prejudice continues to be current on the island."

Santería was the place where the weight of that prejudice seemed a bit lighter. As soon as Isnael had told me what some of the ritual objects looked like—a chain across the doorstep, a wooden or stone vessel filled with sticks and other objects in an entryway, both of which Katherine had at her house, or the multicolored beaded bracelet Isnael wore—I noticed them in the homes of most people I knew in Havana, black or white, foreign or local, old or young. Prohibitions against religion had been dismantled in 1997 and small shops with religious paraphernalia sprouted along the main streets of Old Havana. Sandra was a devotee; she was a child of Changó. Everyone else I interviewed had at least gone to get his or her shells read at some point, a ritual along the lines of getting tarot cards read. Most people had written someone's name on a piece of paper and placed it in the back of a freezer to push that person out of their lives.

Isnael's real goal was not to work at a European expatriate's home, even though his was an enviable gig with a steady flow of *kooks*. Isnael wanted to climb the hierarchy of Santería and make a living in the religion, charging clients, both foreign and local, for spiritual consultation. The Mexicans and Swedes and Italians who came to get initiated provided windfalls and the Cubans stabilized the incomes of *babalawos*, priests. Santería was a growth industry: apart from the believers, there were the Cubans who got initiated as a status symbol, since it cost so much, and the flush foreigners who bragged about initiation back home. So Isnael would work as long as it took him, on a salary of $2 a day, to gather around 65 CUC to buy the materials he'd need for the ceremony to "make saint" and be formally inducted into Santería, plus more to buy new white clothing to wear for the following year so he wouldn't invite any negative energy via his clothes. His *madrina*, to whom he'd apprenticed himself, trained him every weekend and most weekdays. He was convinced that he was looking at a long path, filled with hurdles and trials, but he was equally confident that if he stuck to it, he would be *grande* in religion, he said. Marielena, his *madrina*, had foreseen it; the ancestors had shown her as much. As Isnael told me, the ancestors are sacred in Santería, maybe even more important than the *orishas*. When something is wrong, it might be because someone has asked their dead to meddle in your affairs. When something goes right, thank your ever-present ancestors.

One Wednesday afternoon, I called Katherine's house. Her son picked up the phone.

"Oh! Isnael wanted to tell you something," he said when I identified myself. He shouted for Isnael, and a sharp clack echoed down the line as the receiver dropped to the floor.

I heard Isnael's flip-flops squeaking along the tiles and he picked up the phone. There was a *misa*, a ceremony on Friday at Marielena's house, he said. They were going to bring some ancestors' spirits down to earth through the body of a medium.

"So, if you want to come, you can—it's a $10 *derecho*," he said.

I was curious to see him in his role as religious apprentice, rather than painter-babysitter-bartender, and wondered what the spirits would tell me. The *derecho*, another Cuban acquaintance told me that night, was the fee for the right to participate in the ritual as an outsider. Ten CUC for foreigners, 10 pesos for Cubans. "I can't wait to hear what she tells you," the girl mused. She wrinkled her nose. "The whole place will reek of black people."

/// The asymmetrical room, with low ceilings and yellow paint, was dusty from a renovation that Marielena and her husband had just begun. A scuffed mallet rested in a corner. The living room was empty of furniture except for the dozen chairs that were just starting to fill up, a few offerings, and a small refrigerator that hummed softly in a corner. There was a naked fluorescent lightbulb overhead, the kind that made everyone under it look half-dead.

Years ago, the plot of land that Marielena and her neighbors occupied in the inland Diez de Octubre neighborhood had been someone's backyard or garage. Like the rest of the block, it had been squeezed full of homes accessible by passageways that led past the older street-front houses, the ones with moldings and columns and second-floor open balconies where the wind whisked through drying clothing, and into these home-made houses. Out on the street, pastel plastic buckets hung from pulleys off second and third stories, as in Centro Habana;

women leaned out of windows and refused to come to the street to buy bread or cigarettes. Coins descended; goods went up. On the street, neighbors hovered in doorways smoking and small packs of children flitted from one corner to another, and though these multifamily townhouses hunched shoulder-to-shoulder, more austere than their wealthier Vedado cousins, still there was a resemblance. Past the street, the center of the block was anarchic, heavy. Cinderblock was the reigning medium: Space and ventilation were minimal.

Marielena's home was down a tight fifty-meter hallway. Isnael got quiet as we approached. He'd been telling me more about Santería: As we'd walked through the thick yellow air of 5 PM Vedado, he'd stopped at every *bodega* on the way to the bus stop to ask for *puros*, cigars, because when the spirits come to inhabit someone's body, they like to smoke cigars and drink alcohol, physical pleasures of which they are deprived in the spirit world. The *bodegas* were all out of the peso cigars.

On the bus out from Vedado, as we clung to hot handrails, Isnael had told me that people often got initiated into Santería for reasons that revolved around health—to hedge against a worsening sickness or to thank the deities for helping save someone.

"You can't put a price on health, and any price you could put on it would be low compared to what you get," he said. He had seen a documentary recently about a guy in Africa who had died, he continued. They'd done a ritual on him, fed him something the ancestors had said he could eat in order to cheat death, and he woke back up. To this day, said Isnael, "he's still alive in that little *pueblito* in Africa."

"And you believe this?" I said.

"Yes of course, why wouldn't I? I saw it with my own eyes."

I looked down at the many pairs of legs around ours. This was not what I'd have cited to prove the legitimacy of

Santería's sway over the country. There were too many holes to poke through the veracity of an Internet video. But instead I asked about the flowers.

Throughout the bus ride, he'd cupped his body around a bouquet of flowers he'd bought for the ceremony, and as we walked to Marielena's he carried them with the buds facing down, because "cities are filled with energy, some bad and some good, and these flowers should stay clean of it, not up and open to receive it."

At Marielena's, details like this floated ethereal around the living room as I sat on one side of a lopsided circle of chairs, watching Isnael pull the buds off the flowers and toss them into a bowl. As the group gathered, they gossiped about who had recently had babies and who was selling what on the black market. I had imagined that a Santería ceremony to channel the spirits of the dead through a medium might include dripping candles in dank rooms, hand-holding, maybe some animal sacrifice. This was more like family therapy in a church basement. The small talk came to a close as the last of ten people walked in. Marielena clapped her hands, saying, "OK, everyone, let's get started." Isnael took a chair four people away from me.

I held a wrinkled copy of the words as we began to chant translations of the Hail Mary and the Nicene creed, rhythms familiar from childhood masses with my grandmothers, but these new words repeated in circles, an unbroken spiral as one incantation fed the next, then, without pause, back to the beginning of the first. The edges of the paper were stained dark with finger oil. Isnael recited by heart. Marielena's son, a tall man wearing a crisp green army uniform—he had just been called to participate in a military exercise and would leave for the countryside after the ceremony—drummed a beat on the flipped-over back of a seat cushion. The chanting continued but everyone now switched to call-and-response in Spanish and Yoruba. A pudgy *ahijado* with two earrings— Ariel, son of Mirna, the similarly rotund, fidgety white woman who had convoked this ceremony—clapped an intermittent opposing beat. The whining wail of the leading voice shifted around the room as different people sang the verse.

Marielena sat toward a corner. She wore a skirt made of triangles of brightly colored fabric and her long fingernails wore chipped pink nail polish. She raised her hand to stop the singing. Her chest was rigid. She sucked on the end of a cigar and nodded her head faintly, imperiously. The room shivered with a bruisy quiet. A moth flickered around the lightbulb, pinging as its wings hit the glass. Marielena squinted her eyes. She started pelting Mirna with questions shaped like statements.

"I see . . . I hear noises in your house."

"Luz," Mirna responded, nodding.

"There's an angry spirit. He's rustling around your house, making noises, like, for example, when you think no one is home, *mmmhmmm.* . . . Is that right?"

"Luz."

"That big bang you heard a few weeks ago? You thought it was maybe a car backfiring, or fireworks, but no, no . . . no, it was the spirit."

"Luz," Mirna leaned forward.

Marielena nodded thoughtfully. She detailed the offerings that Mirna could make to placate this angry spirit—food and alcohol by the front door. Once he got his fill, the spirit would leave her family alone. Mirna listened, credence written on her broad face. Isnael looked at Marielena reverently.

The question-and-answer ping-ponged to different people in the circle. Marielena had explained to me earlier, as her devotees had filtered in, that insight came from the spirit she channeled, Francisca, who showed her visions but needed confirmation or denial from the people in the room to guide the visions toward the truth. She consulted nearly everyone for around five minutes each. Then Marielena turned to me.

"What you're doing right now, you didn't study to do it, did you," she murmured as if to herself. "You studied something similar, though."

"Yeah, that's right, kind of," I said, startled. As the words left my mouth, Mirna, seated next to me, nudged me to uncross my legs—crossed arms or legs kept the spirit from touching down in the human world—and whispered that the only answer was *luz*, light, to indicate that Francisca was on the right path. "Luz" or "no."

"*Mmm*," murmured Marielena with a sharp nod. "The shadow of my spirit says that if you truly devote yourself to what you are doing, you will find much success."

A doll in a skirt that matched the one that Marielena wore stared down from her perch atop the refrigerator.

I paused before saying, "Luz."

Her shiny plastic ankles stuck out and her eerily large eyes gazed over my head.

"Cuba is an important place for you," Marielena continued. "But something holds you back from truly committing to being here."

"Luz," I said, nodding. Isnael, two people away from me, tracked my reactions. I was suddenly conscious of trying to keep my cheeks and eyebrows as flat as possible.

"If you stay, Cuba will be good for you," she said. "You should be here, really be here."

Then Marielena began to tell me about a place, a street where row houses lined up and shared walls and had stairs leading up to their front doors. It was vague enough that, on the slide show in my mind, I saw various places that I'd either lived in (college, Mexico City) or visited before (Europe, Vietnam). Really, it could have been anywhere. "Luz," I said hesitantly—I told her it sounded kind of like where I lived in Mexico City. In a room full of Cubans who had never left the island, I was embarrassed to highlight the differences between us. Once I had consciously given her a half-truth, her knowing nod looked fake.

"Yes, of course, it is your home. There is a young man, and he is entering your house," she said. "He is at home in your house. Now he is answering your door."

I didn't know many very young men, and certainly none that would be entering and exiting my house as she'd described. I told her as much.

"It is someone younger than you, like Isnael's age. Who could it be?" Her eyes flicked over to Isnael, and back to me.

I contradicted her vision gingerly, not wanting to upset the balance of power, and asked her who it might be if it wasn't someone I already knew. Perhaps she was referring to Isnael, imposing something lurid on what I had appreciated as a rare platonic dynamic with a Cuban male, an interview subject whose statements weren't spiked with innuendo, and my resentment swelled and grew. Her pause stretched on. The room was quiet and I tried to keep my face impassive.

"She believes," someone on my right murmured. Everyone looked at me, scouring my face for signs of disbelief.

"She believes," Marielena's son said, louder then, as if to dismiss the idea that my belief was just on loan until Francisca proved her omniscience. It's okay if some predictions are slightly off, he seemed to tell me with his eyes. Isnael looked down. And just like that, Marielena's motives were on my mind. I had lied by omission in the name of trying to belong, and she had played along. She seemed smug and everyone stared at me. I felt a saccharine look coming over my face as

I tried to hide my skepticism from Isnael. The absence of my disagreement or affirmation crackled and the hush stretched and grew and I strained not to fidget.

"You'll see, he'll come to you . . . you'll find out who he is soon enough," Marielena said with a shrug to dismiss the point. She moved on to consult with the last two people in the room.

After about an hour's consultation with Francisca, Marielena was quiet. The chanting resumed, this time raucous and less serious than before. It was something between a support group meeting and a festive tribal drum circle; it was not remotely like a séance. I recited phonetically similar phrases in the chorus of the songs and Marielena's son caught me and cracked a joke, pointing and exclaiming something that I didn't catch. Everyone laughed. I smiled and shrugged while clapping. My back and legs felt cramped; I had spent two hours glued to the seat of my uncomfortable metal chair. Every time I tried to find a better position and lifted my knee to cross my legs, Mirna poked my thigh and shook her head. Then she'd lift the edges of her mouth in a taut, conspiratorial smile and offer me a cigarette. It was the only coping mechanism available in the smoky room.

Suddenly, Isnael rose from his seat, shoulders heaving to the beat of the makeshift drum. The jokes stopped. He tossed himself onto the floor and crouched on all fours. His head hung limply down, its crown nearly touching the concrete floor. His body was taken over by tremors. He mumbled unintelligibly as he began to rise to his feet. His knobby knees rattled; he put his hands on them to stabilize himself and stood. He danced a jittery sequence in the middle of the circle. His eyes were squeezed shut and his mouth puckered. He fell to the ground, pounded the floor with his fist, and pushed himself up again. The cycle repeated.

Isnael was no longer the confident kid who just a few hours earlier had marched down the streets of stately Vedado, fake Gucci sunglasses tucked into his hair. A water main near the bus stop had broken, and the sidewalk had puddled with rippling water that made its way down the incline toward the ocean. He'd leapt over it and turned back to offer me his hand. I saw no trace of that self-assured boy. Isnael now was panting, fervent, nearly drooling, an embodiment of something entirely different from the person I knew. It was as if he'd sliced himself in two and here in front of me was the uncouth, the urgent part of him, allowed contact with the world in this room only.

I stopped trying to keep up with the ceremony, stopped chanting and clapping. No one looked at his face but me; no one seemed surprised but me. Isnael's tall, tired-looking, Lycra-clad mother, who had arrived late at Marielena's and hovered in the doorway, clapped along, somber but blank. His trance lasted for ten minutes that felt much longer: The group sang an intense call-and-response, copying Marielena's son in a jagged chorus.

The fridge moaned gently under the beat. Isnael crouched down and pounded the floor again, this time calling for *aguardiente* in a coarse voice. He gurgled it down. Then he asked for blessed water, which Marielena poured on his face, and this woke him up. His head hung toward his sloped shoulders as he returned to his seat, squeezed between Ariel, Mirna's son, and his teenage girlfriend. The singing continued, but tersely, the edges of each verse sharper than before.

After another ten minutes, Mirna started to cry, the unfiltered cigarettes that she had been chain-smoking quivering at her lips. She wiped her face with the back of a clumsy hand.

Three hours into the ceremony now, Francisca came to inhabit Marielena's body. She had been an outside force before, but now Marielena entered a trance. Her posture changed: back straight, head high, eyes lightly but firmly shut, mouth pursed. She sat with her legs wide apart on her seat, one hand on each knee, her multicolored skirt draped over her ample legs. Francisca's face was regal, with an aloofness foreign to Marielena. I had to admit that Marielena's gold teeth and pink fingernails looked different on Francisca. She asked for a cigar and began to chew on it.

Francisca began to speak in a language with repetitive sounds and words that I didn't understand. She drank sweet wine as she ate her cigar down to a nub. After each sip of wine, she smacked her lips a few times. One by one, each person stood in the middle of the circle to consult with Francisca. Each time someone's reality seemed not to match with the spirit version she was seeing, her forehead lined with consternation.

Francisca advised everyone in the room in this Yoruba-Spanish language. I was left to read her actions. Ariel, Mirna's son, appeared to be having sexual trouble; Francisca pulled open the waistband of his pants and blew cigar smoke down them. I gathered that Mirna was reassured that the ghost haunting her house would leave. Isnael, the apprentice, sat against the wall. When it was my turn, Marielena's son translated into Spanish as Francisca told me that I needed a new pen. It had to be a fountain pen and it didn't matter if it worked or not. I was to blow cigar smoke on it and rub it with perfumed water and, if possible, bring it to Marielena to be blessed. The talisman would steer my writing toward success.

When Marielena woke out of her trance, it was nearly one o'clock in the morning. We had been in the room for four hours. After a few more chants, the mass was unceremoniously over. We were all mosquito-eaten from bugs that no one had noticed, our eyes bleary from cigarette smoke.

Someone noted that it was now Valentine's Day, so everyone hugged and kissed, an incongruous festive air slicing
through the fatigue.

Marielena was visibly tired. She cut a loaf of bread,
spread mayonnaise on each piece and, moving slower than she
had earlier, passed around the plate as the group dispersed.
Isnael whispered that I should offer my 10 CUC *derecho* fee to
the doll on Marielena's fridge. I found myself looking more
intently at Isnael than I had five hours earlier, as if I'd find
something I hadn't seen before. Marielena's son asked how
I would get home, since I was the only person who did not
live within a few blocks. If I wanted, he said, he'd make room
in his bed. Suddenly, reason came whooshing back into my
mind. It was late at night and I wasn't sure where I was or
how to get home. The fifteen-minute cab ride between me
and familiar downtown Havana seemed very far. I wanted to
go home and eat cereal on my bed.

Isnael offered to accompany me to the main road to wait
for a taxi or a bus to get me back into my part of town. I often
left alone from Cuban gatherings in remote areas of town,
saying I'd wait at the bus stop, and then called a tourist taxi
on my cell phone. But now Isnael walked with me down the
middle of empty streets. The broken buildings crouched in
the shadows as we moved from one streetlamp's pool of warm
light to another. Incredulous, I asked him what he felt when
the spirit came to him. Tonight was the seventh or eighth
time that he'd been visited by the ancestors, he told me. A few
different spirits had passed through his body.

"You heard when I hit the floor with my fist three times
in a row? That was a different spirit coming in," he explained,
cocking his head and looking at me gamely. We had reached
the main street, which was silent. I stood with one foot on the
cracked curb and one foot in the street.

"But what does it *feel* like?" I persisted. I don't think he understood why I needed an explanation. Santería was so much a part of him and his life that its contradictions didn't interest him. He had framed his life around his religion.

"Nothing, really. I can't remember what I say or do when the spirit is in me, but I know it's something. Marielena doesn't feel anything. She's a real expert. You could pinch her and she wouldn't know." I must have looked still more confused because he continued, gesturing to the sky. "The spirits are everywhere, Julia. They see everything, they have knowledge beyond the human knowledge we have. They see across time, countries, everything. You see the stars up there? How, if they could see us, they'd see Havana, Haiti, Florida; now, years ago, whenever—all at once? It's kind of like that. Of course, when it's in me, I can't understand it because I don't know what I'm seeing. It's like I'm awake but not awake at the same time."

I nodded. After fifteen minutes, a car stopped at my waving hand and I negotiated a price, gave Isnael a hug goodbye, and hopped in. My stomach growled; I hadn't eaten since mid-afternoon. The farther I got from Marielena's house, the more any lingering belief I'd had in her predictions faded.

/// Katherine told me she'd never paid taxes in the United States. She was off the radar, she claimed in rum-sodden conversations we had under the Christmas lights that winked from the rebellious plants in her backyard. When I went to the bathroom, the landscape of her home began to shift and change under my gaze. Spines of books could have been empty, held wads of cash that she didn't trust to either Cuban or U.S. banks; the planters in which indoor palms thrived, the stretched canvases raised four inches off her walls, the antique bureau she'd bought from a secret vintage furniture vendor down the street—everything could hold something else. Then I'd go back outside and we'd resume our conversation about mutual acquaintances or the political situation and she'd wave her hand clumsily and spray ash across her patio.

In spring 2009, the U.S. Congress voted to loosen Bush-era restrictions on Cuban American remittances and travel to the island. Secretary of State Hillary Clinton called U.S. policy toward Cuba "failed" and welcomed an offer for fresh talks with Raúl. President Barack Obama declared to the Summit of the Americas in April that "the United States seeks a new beginning with Cuba." *Maybe he'll drop the embargo*, that dream that everyone insisted would change their material circumstances forever, was whispered quickly and accompanied by crossing of chests or a glance heavenward all across Havana in a chorus of aspiration.

There were more foreigners around, too, tourists and journalists and businesspeople. I ran into a man I'd met on a flight over from Mexico, Mike, a towheaded American businessman in his early thirties who said he'd rather raise children in Cuba than back in Illinois. After bumping into one another in Old Havana, we walked down side streets past the back entrances of tourist restaurants where trios played Buena Vista Social Club songs. He knew a spot where we could buy beer at the usual $1 rate rather than the Old Havana $2 markup, so we made a few turns and bought a beer each at an unmarked door. He was laying the groundwork to start an import-export company under the humanitarian loophole of the embargo. He wanted to be on the ground "before the floodgates open," he said. He traced the life he envisioned: a house on the other side of the bay, where there was more space, a simpler life than those we'd live in the States, community, children who'd play stickball in the streets the way his parents had. There was a Cuban girlfriend hovering behind his statements, though Mike never directly mentioned her. I told him vaguely of the interviews I conducted, though I knew, even as the words flipped out of my mouth, that without a journalist's visa I should have been more tight-lipped.

"Meet me at the Hotel Nacional at 7:30. It's important. Make the time. I will check this email again at 6:00 to make sure you got this and will be there. I have some information for you," Mike emailed me a few days later. A second note: "I can't tell you over email. Please don't tell anyone I'm being cryptic."

I waited on one of the couches on the patio under the Hotel Nacional's soaring pink ceilings. When Mike arrived, he stood over me and looked around. "Down there. On the bluff, where it's less visible," he said, motioning for me to follow him. The ocean glistened beyond where we walked, through the grassy pathways that led to the cannons on the Nacional's bluff above Twenty-Third and *malecón*.

"Look, I didn't mean to freak you out with my email," he began. "It's just that the other day, while we were walking in Old Havana, a contact of mine saw us. They're on to you."

I stared at him.

"This guy I know, he's plugged into the CDR. He said they have a whole file on you. They know you're doing interviews with . . . with *jineteras*, right? Yeah, yeah, *jineteras*. I can't be seen with you."

"Well, but wait. What do you mean? Am I in danger? Are my sources? Could my visa be revoked?" The air seemed to have stopped moving around us.

Mike shook his head. "Just keep it quiet and be careful. This is life in Cuba right now. There's too much going on. Don't stop, for God's sake, don't stop. Just, maybe, maybe lay off the sex workers."

He left before I did and after fifteen minutes staring at the ocean I walked the mile or two back home in a night so humid that the streetlights seemed to make pink polka dots on the avenues. American "tourists" had come to Havana with financial and technical support for political dissidents, had come to try to assassinate Fidel, had come with dubious intentions and an overwhelming sense of grandiosity that stemmed from what Joan Didion called, in her 1987 book *Miami*, "a more fluid atmosphere, one in which the native distrust of extreme possibilities that tended to ground the temperate United States in an obeisance to democratic institutions seemed rooted, if at all, only shallowly." If in Miami that rooting was shallow, here in Cuba it was nonexistent. Extreme possibilities were all there were in Havana and this, for temperate Americans, was an intoxicant. We either lived in the pages of a Graham Greene novel or were consumed with prosaic gestures of daily life gritty enough to have been erased long ago in the logical States. Katherine was rumored to cooperate with the Cuban secret service, the cost, it was said, of being allowed to live in Havana. That Mike had veiled motives and was trying to manipulate me felt as true as the possibility that he was overwhelmed with paranoia and intent on spreading it thin. Grandiosity was, in my case at least, chased with the quick throb of realistic inconsequence.

Sometimes there was something of relief in the surrender that Havana forced on privileged foreigners. You couldn't eat what you wanted to eat, *porque no hay*, there wasn't any, and you couldn't visit a neighborhood with new buildings because it didn't exist. Every car, townhouse, staircase, and avenue kept the patina of a city that had given itself to the passage of time and to which I was of no consequence. The people around me were who I knew them to be or they wore masks; someone was reporting on me and though I could compose theories, I had no way to firmly learn who.

/// Isnael was blaring Enrique Iglesias's silky voice through the house as he worked the next few times I saw him. Reggaeton, his music of choice, was roundly prohibited at Katherine's house due to its filthy lyrics. Iglesias, or what Isnael called "la música romántica," was a close second. Isnael was in the process of swiping a sheer silver paint on all of the walls.

"Did you find a pen?" he asked me one afternoon.

I hadn't, I told him, which wasn't entirely true. I'd looked at two underground vintage shops and hadn't seen anything: Havana, I sensed, was rife with old fountain pens, an ocean of them under the skin of what was technically "for sale," sitting in cups on desks in back rooms of Miramar houses and buried in drawers in Old Havana apartments, but I hadn't seen one yet. Still, I wanted to go back to see Marielena again with him anyway, I said, if that was okay. We agreed to go the following week after work.

As it turned out, he'd hardly seen her since the ceremony a few months earlier, he told me as we retraced our steps out of Vedado. He had not made saint yet. He'd been working hard and trying to save, but every time he got close he'd splurge on a new pair of shoes or taking a girl out. He knew what girls liked, see, so it was hard, he confessed, for him to avoid dating altogether. Dates were expensive, what with club cover charges and drinks, so he tried to keep it casual, take a girl out once, have a fling, drop her before it got too serious and she expected more: gifts, dinners, wine. And somewhere along the way Isnael had realized that he liked things, too, and experiences—what money could buy. He liked to go to El Túnel, the club in La Víbora where government nightlife promoters promised weekend nights that lasted into daylight, and wait in the slam of perfumed people outside and know that if he got to the front of the line, he could pay his own way in. He liked to buy himself new sunglasses when his broke. He liked to treat his mother to a pizza if she got hungry while they were out. Yet these activites all depleted his resources and slowed him down, so he was determined now to be either working, at home sleeping in the room he shared with his mother at the end of the alley a block over from Marielena's, or on the bus between the two.

As soon as we arrived, Marielena again shooed me into a chair and Isnael into the kitchen, this time to help her strain a bean soup she had made for dinner. The upstairs half of her house was tight with ceilings low enough that I watched my head. Isnael stooped as he stood at the stove and clattered the bowls he rinsed for us. Marielena said she remembered my last visit but wore the distracted smile of someone who could be lying. After ten minutes of idle chatter, Marielena complimented my Spanish—she'd hardly heard me speak last time, she said—and nodded over at Isnael.

"This one over here wants to learn English," she said as Isnael served soup and sat down.

I raised my eyebrows. I had never heard Isnael utter a word of English.

He ate a spoonful of soup and glanced away. "I want to speak two more languages by the time I'm thirty." Spanish, English, and maybe Portuguese. Though Chinese would be the most useful, he said solemnly, if he wanted to be the next president of Cuba.

There was a momentary silence. From within the hierarchies of Santería, I suddenly saw, the hierarchies of Cuba seemed less rigid, more scalable to Isnael. In his world, the world that mattered to him, there were less firmly demarcated boundaries between concrete and abstract power. But there they were, and vertical hierarchies in Cuba were solid as a pyramid with a Castro-shaped capstone at the top. A *Presidente Isnael* seemed even less probable to me than an Isnael who could see the future.

It had always been community that made Havana feel magical: Webs of people enabled the odd coincidences that felt mystical to me. Santería was a part of what contributed to the sense of community in Cuba, but more important: the Cuban system itself had created it. With unreliable institutions and a vast distance between, as Ernest Hemingway would have said, the mere players and the owners, informal social structures among citizens who didn't rank on the hierarchy picked up the slack. Community stood behind all religions, and so religion, even when Santería receded into the background, appeared to weave through nearly everything in Havana. This, not well-fed spirits, was what made Havana inherently religious, this tension between the providential and prosaic, between being open to new experiences and staying on my guard, was what made me feel so engaged in Havana, what kept me coming back.

"What president?" Marielena asked with a sharp laugh as she ladled more soup into his bowl. "Those old, white men will die and other old, white men will take their place."

/// "You know there are always turns in the road with Cuba but in the end you will have everything you want—I am positive of this," Mike wrote in our next email exchange, the last we would have while I lived in Cuba. "You and I both know it won't be easy, but we'll be there."

This, my foreign-ness and "being there," was what unlocked Havana's potential and coincidence to me. Even so, a few months later I would wind up dating a younger man. It would be years before I would connect him to Marielena's prophecy. We weren't together for long, just long enough that he answered my door once or twice.

6

TARZANS AND CIRCUS CLOWNS

ADRIÁN AND ADELA

I try to, at the hour of showing my reality, preserve its ambivalence,
because that is the purpose of the artistic discourse. Other
discourses—religious, political—have different goals, but the base of
artistic pursuit is ambivalence and complexity.

–Cuban filmmaker Fernando Pérez

If you asked a naïve twenty-year-old Miles Davis fan what a young jazz musician's day-to-day might resemble, he'd probably describe Adrián's life. When he was in town, Adrián squatted at a Vedado apartment that an uncle of his, a professor at the university, had left vacant for a few years while teaching at another Caribbean university. He had moved in at age twenty-three, a year and a half ago, and taken charge of its upkeep. There were two mattresses on the apartment's floor: a double in the bedroom and a single in the living room where his friends often crashed. The only other pieces of furniture were an upright piano, a small circular table and two stools, and an end table next to his bed with a framed photograph of himself and his girlfriend, who lived there with him. She'd helped him paint the place the color of old Pepto Bismol. The color was discounted the weekend they'd gone to the store and Adrián wanted to get the job done before leaving for Europe.

His fridge held cool water, a half-full bottle of vodka and a half-eaten bar of chocolate, pasta sauce, rice, and a thumb-sized packet of pot. When friends stopped by, mostly other musicians or art students, Adrián liked to light a shisha he'd brought from Morocco and sit for a while on the large patterned throw pillows he'd bought in Spain, laughing over what they'd all said the last time they'd smoked. Sometimes they'd turn on the twenty-inch flat-screen he'd picked up in the Dominican Republic. The walls were bare but for a moody, black-and-white photo of him that hung in one corner of the living room—the same image from his MySpace music profile, which he maintained on hotel computers every week or so.

Every day, Adrián woke up and practiced. Recent afternoons he'd been recording soundtracks for a local *telenovela* for 5 *kooks* a session, which was crappy pay but curried favor with the right people. If he wasn't working, he went to auditions, among them for a steady gig on a cruise ship. He didn't get it—they'd wanted someone over fifty. Gray hair, the Buena Vista Social Club type. In the early evening, a few friends, mostly musicians or art students, would stop by, and then Adrián would leave for his evening gig, meet up with people after, come home, sleep late, warm up on his piano, and on and on. The year of upward mobility for Adrián was 2009. That year alone, he'd done a concert for a rich guy's New Year's Eve party in the Dominican Republic, a quick run with the showcase group Hijos de Buena Vista in Russia, and a five-week tour in France and North Africa with a salsa singer's band. He'd saved most of what he'd earned, 250 Euros per show playing piano with the *salsero's* band; he walked everywhere while abroad and returned to Havana with toys. A Swatch watch from Europe, Ray-Bans and the TV from the Dominican Republic, a white MacBook with a French keyboard.

Adrián had been studying at music-oriented schools since he was seven years old, when he scored well in an aptitude test and earned one of around fifteen coveted spots in a local music school. From there, he'd tracked into the music middle and high schools. He was right now supposed to be attending the Instituto Superior de Arte, the bucolic art university that Castro had set down on what had been the Havana Country Club's golf course, a corollary to the sixties mandate that radios play local music and galleries show local artists. This was the university to which Carlos had applied. Its mellow hills and filled-in sand traps held facilities for visual arts, dance, music, and theater that culled students from around the country, but Adrián had begged out of class to go on a national tour with one of Pablo Milanes's daughters a year ago and had been returning in only the most cursory way since. School trained classical. Adrián wanted pop or avant-garde.

He was trying to launch his own jazz quartet, a group of musicians that he'd headline. All had been friends since elementary school. All spent most of their days playing music, talking about music, reading books on music, listening to music. All spoke with the aspirational language of people with contingency plans and professional networks and bank accounts with an accumulation in them, not just the dregs of their last direct-deposit government paycheck in pesos. The sax player had just taken a job abroad. Adrián was testing a replacement. If he could get the band up and running, Adrián said one afternoon with the easy confidence of the privileged, maybe he'd stick around Havana more, tour with musicians less. "You know how the world likes the Cubans who live here, not there," he told me with a shrug and a gesture toward the rest of the world.

The band's third concert would happen in three hours at La Zorra y el Cuervo, the jazziest of jazz clubs in Havana, a cave of burgundy velvet and dark wood entered through a vintage phone booth on Twenty-Third. Adrián was informal about dates—he showed up an hour late and was infuriatingly cheerful for interview appointments, sent me a text message at seven-fifty on a Monday night to say he'd be playing at eight—but this time he'd invited me three days in advance to go with the band to their show. La Zorra y el Cuervo was a few blocks from Adrián's apartment. He hoped it'd be jammed with the tourist crowd that set aside at least one night of their Havana package tours to hear Latin jazz.

The new saxophone player would meet us there, but the drummer had just knocked on the door with the friend who used to play sax with them. We waited only for the bassist.

Adrián flicked on the TV and streamed a video of Brazilian funk artist Ed Motta, who sounded like a Portuguese blend of Stevie Wonder and Jamiroquai, as he wound cords into loose loops. Nailé, who had just returned from Spain with the Cuban pop musician for whom she played drums, sat cross-legged on the floor as the two boys began to pack bass, amps, Adrián's keyboard. She held a stray guitar in her lap, steady against the rubber of her tennis shoes, and tapped on it with her thumb and pinkie fingers as she shook her head in rhythm with the swingy, synthesized songs. She had shaved her head a few months ago and now kept her hair at less than an inch long. I sat in a chair next to her, my elbows on my knees.

One song ended and another began, with a faster beat and an electric guitar that did occasional solos between bouts of Motta's singing. The tiny man on the screen was hugely overweight, the stage was color-blocked, and the band wore pink-striped and polka-dot ties like R&B–crooning Pee-wee Hermans. The scene started to resemble a cliché even as it began to occur, a scene from a movie about Afro-Cuban musicians with ambition and talent to spare, young people *going places* in a harsh country, but the energy was genuine: Adrián and the saxophonist paused their packing to watch the screen. No light illuminated the living room but the TV and a square of white from the bare bulb in Adrián's bed-room. Nailé's earrings dangled, pendulums in time with the music. They should try to steal this rhythm, she said, try it out sometime and see what they could do with it. She jumped to her feet. CDs from a precariously placed disc holder on the table rained down with a clack and arrayed themselves on the floor like rainbowed fish scales. No one looked. The two boys had taken their shirts off, because why get them sweaty and damp, and the light from the TV glinted on their shiny chests. Adrián danced lankily. "*Taka taka taka-ta-ta*, see? Like that. *Taka taka taka-ta-ta*," he said. It was more electronic than anything they'd done before, Nailé said to me, but what the hell. Experimentation was half the point.

When the song ended and the packing resumed, Adrián told me that once, when he was sixteen, he had grabbed at a loose electric cable when he tripped in the street. The cur-rent went in the palm of his hand, through just below his right armpit, and out his right foot before he let go. A stiff, dark, spidery scar ran along the palm of his hand and splin-tered out in rays at his wrist; he had a wide, kidney-shaped scar on the side of his chest. The sole of his foot was singed two shades darker than his skin and his toes were wonky, which was also why he didn't exercise, he added. He wore his hair in a large afro that he twisted into thick spikes like black meringue. His hair was not crazy because he had been electrocuted, but his hair was crazy and he had been electrocuted, he said.

They didn't fill La Zorra y el Cuervo that night. It wasn't empty, either: Around twenty foreigners showed up, plus a few teachers from the Instituto Superior de Arte. The club was cold with the meat-locker air conditioning of fancy establishments in tropical climates, and Adrián grinned and mugged with the microphone as he introduced each song to the tourists, who'd all brought sweaters. When he played, his head seemed to loosen from his body, waggling above the piano, painting the air with the thick soft tips of his hair.

I sat with Adrián's old friend, who would play for a year at a luxury hotel in Southeast Asia. He was leaving in a few weeks and though he would miss "blowing up along with the band," he couldn't turn down the promise of financial stability. His salary provided more money in a month than what his parents made, combined, in two years.

/// If Adrián was going to spend more time in Havana, he was going to do it on his terms: in an apartment he'd bought where he didn't have to worry about rehearsing too loud or too much and pissing off the neighbors. He wanted to play with his quartet, traverse the city not in *guaguas*, buses, or *máquinas* but only in private gypsy cabs, or buy his own car, if he could, and eat at places like the Jazz Café. The Jazz Café at the intersection of Paseo y *malecón* had a jovial host who approached the table when local regulars came in, sat down, didn't look at the menu, and instead asked for a screwdriver or a whiskey, and whatever was freshest from the *agro* that morning. The 10-*kook* minimum consumption bill that kept other Cubans out was always waived. Dinner and two drinks usually came out to around 7 or 8 CUC.

Adrián was the guy playing piano at the Jazz Café every Monday night while those people came in and out. He and his new band weren't a name yet and they didn't have the recognition to play their original songs as regulars anywhere, so he played Cuban standards with a house band and took whatever else came along. Even so, the money he was earning was starting to place him in the category of the people who didn't need to use the menu or pay covers at restaurants like Jazz Café.

To Adrián, Cuba was just like anywhere else, with an elite that had sorted out how to work the system and a large portion of the populace that hadn't had either the conditions or the savvy to navigate the maze. He hadn't been born into anything, he was quick to point out: his parents were black university professors who'd never had a ton of money. His ascent demonstrated something about success in Havana, that it still existed and could be achieved through hard work.

Purchasing an apartment would demonstrate something else, something about Adrián's investment and confidence in Cuba's future. This was why Adrián was saving up. The sort of place he wanted would cost him around $20,000 under the table, with the deed trading hands via a sham marriage, probably. "I'm getting ready for whatever's coming next. Learning from everything, just in case," he said. "Plus I'm exploding."

Nonchalance-encased yearning was a trademark of Havana's cultural elite. These were people who spent a few months outside the country every year; people who summered in Spain or conspicuously didn't discuss the woes of being on peripatetic band tours—one night here, two nights there, three nights in Madrid or Antibes if they were lucky. At gallery openings when their artwork was shown in Switzerland

and Mexico, small knots of Europeans or Latin Americans formed around them because these people, in Diesel jeans and trim blazers, weren't what a Cuban was supposed to look like. They booked airplane tickets on computers at the Meliá Cohiba, got 2-*kook* mani-pedis from women who made house calls, kept haunches of black-market *jamón Serrano* on kitchen counters, worked out in the back room of a Miramar house where guys who rode with the Cuban national team taught spinning on rusty Schwinn stationary bikes. They drank vodka, not rum, and their Wednesday nights were often spent with a bottle of it and a friend or two, talking about art and books and politics and life. They lent each other essay collections by Dave Hickey, Taschen tomes on contemporary art, mp3s of musicians like Ed Motta. They didn't go out much to Cuban bars or to tourist bars; they went to each other's houses, to parties where furniture slid to the outskirts of the living room to make space for a dance floor so that attendees could finally dance salsa, do a casino round. They did wine nights to which each invitee was expected to bring a decent bottle, usually purchased at the diplomat grocery store or the Meliá wine shop because the black-market vendors sold only the mediocre wines served by all-inclusive hotels. They were coolly disinterested in what mainstream Cubans did, but a significant swath of the rising cultural elite, like Adrián, corroborated one success of *eltriunfodelarevolución*, always spoken as if it were one word—the egalitarian arts education system that had made them. They were also evidence of a political and artistic reality.

People like Adrián worked their way up the professional ladder inside Cuba first, playing in local bands or showing in local galleries until they were noticed by a visiting international music producer or curator. Then, if they were ambitious, they'd begin to travel abroad, to collect exit visas procured through the National Union of Cuban Writers and Artists or another MinCult entity with ease proportionate to their prestige. Abroad, they'd be the face of a new Cuba, well-dressed and talented, living proof that the *yanqui* newspaper articles on dissidents and poor people who fished cans from the garbage to make toys for tourists weren't the only Cuban reality. They were proof that exit visas were, in fact, granted, proof that the education system worked, at least for some. A portion of their earnings, whether through foreign record contracts or sales of canvases to visiting art collectors, was paid in taxes to the state. All but a very few kept apartments in Havana, even when they got foreign grants to live abroad for a spell. Most made sure to visit Cuba every eleven months, because if they stayed out of the country for longer, they would be seen by the law as having defected. That benefitted no one—not the artist, not the government. Someone who defected was an immigrant. Someone who kept residency was a Cuban.

And so they discussed dreams and plans with alluring ease, as if the constructions of success would rise out of concrete and I-beams as easily as the words floated from their mouths. Their phrasing hid the bite of failure, no hedging or trailed-off sentences. They didn't bring up having lived in an Old Havana *barbacoa*, or whether they'd ever seen someone stabbed on a street corner because whoever did it just couldn't take the degradation, the policeman every two corners who kept ordering you to show your *carnet* though his eyes glinted with recognition when he saw you. Many of them moved. In nice neighborhoods like Vedado or Miramar, and all the way out to Siboney and Nautico—neighborhoods that held embassies and foreign businesses and the arts and sports schools—shoulders were straighter, slang was less vulgar, and privacy was respected. These were the neighborhoods where foreigners stayed in *casas*, neighborhoods that bewitched with easy hospitality and attractive residents.

Adrián wanted an apartment in a good neighborhood, but not one of the foreigner-ridden, expensive ones. Nuevo Vedado, maybe, where modernist apartment houses hid in the low hills just behind downtown Vedado, or a nice house in El Cerro, where he'd grown up, or La Víbora, where apartments were great and still cheap. "And soon, before things change," Adrián told me as he rolled a joint in his apartment a few days after his concert. "Ninety percent of young people here don't do anything, they're just waiting in their houses for a change to come, but they aren't preparing themselves for it."

I paused, thinking. "But what are they supposed to do? I mean, the system here doesn't exactly—"

Adrián shook his head as he interrupted me. "Look, at the end, if you don't do well, it's your own damn problem." His impatience thickened the air. "It's not the system's fault. The doctors, the teachers, the ones that are really, really good, they live a good life. It's the bad ones that complain.

"That's what I don't like about so many Cubans," he continued. "Even the educated ones, they talk so much shit about Cuba, but they've never even seen what it's like outside. It's hard out there, too. In a different way, but it's hard."

He lit the joint, took a hit, and passed it to me. "Bro, you're an asshole, you think you have some right to a good life and lots of money just because you went to college? No, you were given the chance to study and now it's on you to make it yourself. Beyond the Revolution or socialism or capitalism, I'm talking about opportunities. At the end, everyone who makes it in anything in any system is good at what he does. Don't talk shit, don't complain, because in the end, every system gives anyone the opportunity to use it."

I shrugged and we moved on.

Adrián would never admit to me that he felt lucky. To admit that his success was partially the product of having the right skill set in the right country under the right cultural policy, I thought, destabilized him. If his success was due to his own enterprise, then he'd earned his toys; the narrative he was constructing about himself, his life, his work, and his place in Havana held.

There was a looseness about Adrián that made him credible when he said that he'd never really considered defecting on any of his trips abroad, a looseness that I thought could only really survive in Cuba. Every time he came back from a long trip, it was as if Adrián breathed deeply for the first time since he'd left. He earned money abroad and spent it at home: to support his girlfriend, buy his parents a new air conditioner if theirs broke, take taxis. He'd miss Havana too much, he said, the *resolviendo*, the Cuban women and their combination of dependence and independence that existed nowhere else, the crazy, romantic alchemy of Havana. I'd felt that detail, too, every day since I'd moved here: walking down the hill from the Hotel Nacional toward the *malecón* on a hot, dry, windy afternoon, smelling the salt air and watching how the sea seemed to press against the cars that sped around the curve.

No, Adrián talked about travel and foreign jobs but he'd only ever live in Havana. He hated how polite people were outside Cuba—he called it fake—and couldn't understand why socioeconomic classes were kept so rigidly apart. It struck him as hypocritical that people acted one way at work and a different way at home. "There's *doble moral* here, too, but at least it's the sort that I understand. You have to use your head in a different way. Other people, like French people, can't handle chaos. Cubans react more *suave*. In Cuba, autonomy doesn't exist," he said, one of the grand contradictory statements that exposed how conscious he was that I was interviewing him.

Adrián's notion of himself held as long as he was onstage in one way or another. It cracked when he was forced back into his younger self, such as when we ran into an old mentor on the street that afternoon as we left his apartment, a guy who played now with the famous salsa orchestra Charanga Habanera. He retreated into momentary reflection, a sentence on how far he'd come and how it was all doing something he loved.

He shook himself normal again, a dog waggling off the water, and suggested we grab a mojito at the Hotel Nacional.

/// There was a Charanga Habanera song on every DJ's spin list that year. The song is sung by a Cuban man, speaking to a girlfriend who's just gone to the other side of the Straits. She says Miami's crazy, he croons. She feels good and she has money and the nice car she always dreamed of, but she can't find the gossip, the flavor of Havana. What she doesn't have is all over the screen in the music video: dirty dancing in bikinis by a clean-ish pool, a pile of kids chicken-fighting and laughing, girls giggling together while sunbathing. She sits on an immaculate white couch, alone, a remote on the coffee table, a cordless phone in her hand as she talks to him. He rubs it in: "Tu llorando en Miami, yo gozando en la Habana." You're crying in Miami, I'm enjoying Havana. In the chorus, he asks her:

> *Cuentame como te ha ido*
> *Si has conocido la felicidad.*
> *Cuentame como te va*
> *Yo por aqui, muy bien, tu por alla, que bola?*

Tell me, how have things been going
Have you found happiness?
Tell me how you are.
Me over here, I'm really good,
You over there, what the hell?

The song is uncommonly catchy. Dance floors filled every time the intro horn line sounded at any party. The last line of the chorus emerged like a mantra, its last words, "Que bola?" shouted with arms in the air in mock confusion.

Adela knew how to dance to this song. She didn't look like she should—unlike the stars of the music video, she had neither classic dark Spanish looks nor mixed-race skin, but long, thin, light brown hair and the start of a wrinkle between her hazel eyes because every time she got worked up talking about politics or philosophy, which was often, she furrowed her brow. The wrinkle had been developing since she was around nineteen, when I met her. Now she was twenty-four and a recent graduate of the University of Havana.

The sentiment of "Gozando en la Habana" agreed with Adela. Adela was the most patriotic Cuban I knew who wasn't a seventy-year-old *campesino*. We'd met talking politics at the university, where we'd spend hours with a group that included a Mexican philosophy student and a German political historian, discussing politics under the weeping fig trees in the grand porticos of the university buildings. Inside, the wooden desks had been painted so many times that the surfaces were soft, and still they wore the names of their favorite students. There was little breeze in the classrooms, the bathroom toilets had no running water, and the tank with the bucket that you were to use to flush manually was rarely full. The sense of noble knowledge being imparted clashed with the stench of piss and cigarette smoke. But outside, in the bright patios with sloppily landscaped trees gone to elegant riot, students sat on benches and debated politics, philosophy, art theory, literature.

The United States was thick in its engagement with Iraq, which loosed Adela's policy perspectives. Americans invaded foreign countries whenever it was convenient, using conscripts who "volunteered" for service after sitting in putrid pools of entrenched poverty, wars voted for by a "democracy" of wealthy white men whose children were safe in private universities. Americans used poorly paid workers in factories abroad to make products that were discarded by Americans after mere weeks, and were then sold to the ranks of middle-class climbers in whatever country the product had originated while American bosses raked in the cash. A country that kept to itself was the only ethically defensible nation. A country that exported doctors rather than businessmen, this was the philosophically correct policy.

Adela rarely grew impatient, rowdy, or rude while debating. She usually laughed at what she deemed stupid, a high-pitched giggle reserved for an ill-considered claim. She detached only when whoever she spoke with didn't address her points but instead began to point toward Cuban policy. And even then, it was a simple shift in the focus of her eyes, in whether she looked at you and furrowed her brow or glazed into the distance. She hated feeling plucked from a case, as if people were marveling at her amid relics of other obsolescences from years long past, she later told me: look, a *young Communist*! She hardened against people who thought they knew her. She was unclassifiable. She hadn't joined the Union of Young Communists, though eleven of the thirteen sociology students who graduated with her belonged to it, because she fancied herself an "independent militant," too ardent even for the UJC. The UJC was filled with impostors who just wanted better social service assignments after graduation. "The selection isn't how it was before," she complained. "They used to pick the vanguard, young people who were really critical, who questioned. The young people today who show off their UJC cards, they have no questions. They don't even read the local press, much less *El País* to get another perspective."

Adela wanted to be like Haydée Santamaría, whose apartment had been the Havana haven of the radical youth movement under Batista, who fought alongside the men at the Moncada barracks on July 26, 1957, who later headed the Casa de las Américas cultural center, who supported cultural icons like Silvio Rodríguez and his *trovadores*. Santamaría had recognized talent, art, passion, love of homeland, and a commitment to social justice. She was a role model. Adela cited the 5-peso entry to museums and free concerts as Santamaría's inheritance but left out the part where she committed suicide on July 26, 1980. She was fifty-eight.

Adela had just moved to Tarará, a beach town twenty minutes by car from East Havana and the first of the *playas del este* beaches. After graduating from the University of Havana, she'd been sent there to complete her first year of social service. Chinese teens had descended in clusters on the country to learn Spanish, part of a recent agreement between Fidel Castro and Hu Jintao. Adela had been asked to teach a group of twenty of them for a year, and though she'd politely declined—she preferred to perform her duty within Havana, at an editorial house, say, or the university—the "asking," as it turned out, was really telling.

Adela had never lived in a *beca*, government student housing, before. Throughout her childhood, her mother, a well-connected woman with the dyed red hair of an aging pinup from whom Adela had inherited lively eyes and wide, high cheekbones, had pulled strings to get her out of the *escuelas al campo*, the harvest volunteer work that all Cuban schoolchildren had to do. And when it came time for high school, Adela's allergies were bad enough to get out of being *becada*.

Everyone who went to one of the high schools that tracked into the University of Havana had to live in a *beca*, a dormitory outside Havana, unless they were artists, sports-men, or infirm. The only two city high schools that tracked into the University of Havana were where the second-tier athletes and the kids with a medical reason not to live in the *becas* studied. Top athletes in sports like baseball, track and field, and boxing, in which Cuba consistently ranked at the Olympics, lived in their own sports facility on the out-skirts of town and were expected eventually to compete at the Pan-American Games while the lesser athletes went to college. So the ranks of sailors, horseback riders, and prac-titioners of other sports in which Cuba rarely placed were swollen with the children of the elite. Doctor's notes were, for the right people, also procurable.

Through high school and then college, Adela stayed in Havana, with her mother and stepfather and older brother in leafy Miramar, with her own bedroom and her books: Voltaire, Marx, Nietzsche. Adela talked about authors as if she'd had dinner with them the night before. She attended the annual February book fair with saved money to buy spe-cific, sought-after books from small Argentine and Spanish presses. Her most treasured tomes lived on a shelf in the old mahogany headboard that took up most of her bedroom: Julio Cortázar, Jorge Luis Borges, Jorge Mañach.

She brought some of those books with her to Tarará, but there was no way to bring everything to the small room she shared with another teaching student. More important, with only one day off every two weeks and no quick way to get into Havana, Adela couldn't go to the library or to the museums or the film festivals that had sustained her since high school.

"I feel imprisoned," she complained to me over the phone a few weeks into the assignment. "It's as if they had told you, after you graduated from Georgetown, that you had to go to Florida to inspect houses for mosquitoes. What? Why? Is this what I've been prepared for, what I've studied for all these years? Is this all you expect of me?"

I laughed.

"The installations are nice, imagine, they were all ready for the Chinese," she said. "I was sad when I got here but I tried to contain myself. One girl was crying, crying, she couldn't stop, she just had the phone glued to her ear and was crying. What could I say to her; I didn't even know her! I laugh so I don't cry about the whole thing."

/// In the early months of 1959 after *eltriunfodelarevolución*, Che Guevara had holed up in an abandoned mansion in Tarará, complaining of sickness and exhaustion, asthma that wouldn't let up. Guevara's choice of accommodations in the suburban beach town, billed by the *New York Herald Tribune* in a 1952 article entitled "Cuban Vacation More Than Just Havana Nights" as "an exclusive summer colony, every resident being a member of the Tarara Yacht Club," was a source of derision among some, including a journalist who published a story revealing Che's new home as one of Tarará's poshest estates. In response, Guevara published an open letter to editor and Compañero Carlos Franqui of the *Revolución* newspaper to say that he "had to occupy a home of one of the members of the old regime because my salary of $125 as an official in the Red Army does not permit me to rent one large enough to house the people who accompany me."

Later, Tarará became the locus of Cuba's medical diplomacy. In the nineties, the town erected dormitories to house children from areas downwind of the 1986 Chernobyl nuclear disaster while Cuban doctors treated them for exposure. After the Special Period, in the era of Hugo Chavez and tightening bonds with Venezuela, poor Latin Americans came to Tarará for eye surgeries funded jointly by the two countries. And in 2007, the town began to host a few hundred of the two thousand Chinese high school graduates who arrived every year to train as translators. They were taught by young college graduates in their social service year who fit Cuba's public relations persona: racially diverse, energetic, good-looking, Communist.

Though she didn't want to be in Tarará, Adela fit the requirements. She lived in a small peach-colored house behind the hulking yellow student dormitories, where T-shirts could be spied from the highway, drying out of windows, with five other young women and a cocker spaniel. The window in the room she shared overlooked an empty blue swimming pool with dried brown palm fronds clustered at the bottom. Beyond, she could see a broad swath of sea. At night she heard nothing but the waves and the palm trees that flopped in the wind.

There were aspects of her imprisonment that Adela enjoyed. The view. Independence from her family. Instead of being strong-armed by cohabitation into talking to her mother at home, Adela spoke with her once a week on the phone and saw her on a day off every two weeks. It felt so adult. She got a computer in her classroom with access to the Internet; she read the Spanish newspaper *El País* daily and posted thoughtful quotes from Simone de Beauvoir and John Keats on her instant message status. She learned about China, whose instant noodles and spicy sauces filled Cuban supermarket shelves. Adela would rather have experienced these things because of something she'd chosen to do, but within her annoyed resignation was a nugget of excitement.

"You have no idea how hard it can be, with the different codes we have," she wrote me in an email. "They express themselves differently in every way. They're introverted, but if they open up, they seem even stranger because how they think about absolutely everything is entirely different. Their parents teach them that they're little emperors, the hope of the family." In one of the first Spanish exercises she'd assigned, a dialogue she'd instructed them to pair up for, her students had each written both sides of the assignment alone. "Imagine it! One person, reciting: Hola. *Hola.* ¿Como estas? *Yo estoy muy bien, ¿y tu?*"

Though Adela had known foreign students before, they had always been one or two within a classroom of dozens of Cubans. She'd never been a minority in a room before and she seemed to be squeezing something from the experience. Adela learned to use chopsticks to eat her rice and beans, and a favorite student taught her to make dumplings, stiff hats of flour that she filled with spiced onion and chard and presented to me on a plate one afternoon. She ate tofu: slimy and a little bland, she said, but kind of good. She reported these cultural experiences solemnly. There were so many different ways of being, she seemed to say with every observation. I thought back to our multinational group of acquaintances in college, walking together in the dark morning of May Day from the University to the broad, open Plaza de la Revolución, where Fidel would give his speech, and wondered what she'd observed about me.

But with only two days off per month, Adela missed the December and February film festivals and got only a slice of an afternoon at the book fair. And since Tarará was a place of governmental mission, anyone who visited her needed to get a special permit from the police. She wasn't allowed to invite me or any other foreigner to visit her, even if she spoke to a higher-up and vouched for me. When she offered to sneak me in toward the end of her year there, other resentments bubbled out in the tone with which she used to cite Haydée Santamaría. I spent ten minutes in the compound: Adela had flirted aggressively with a teenaged guard and I slipped in on the promise that I was Mexican and definitely not a *yanqui* and I would be inside for just long enough for us to change into our swimsuits. After touring the winding roads of what was essentially a suburb surrounded by an iron fence, we returned to the beach to sit in the sand. It was too chilly to swim. Offerings that Santería devotees had made to Yemayá, the powerful female *orisha* of the seas, had washed up on the shore: squash, a bloated watermelon, chicken feathers twisted among clumps of dried seaweed.

Adela was troubled that Fidel, the intellectual and char-ismatic dinosaur whose continuing dictatorship she had toler-ated out of allegiance to and respect for what he had initially accomplished, had replaced himself with Raúl, a military man who was as much of a dinosaur as his brother, less intellec-tual, and with zero charisma. She didn't understand why Raúl had then fired Felipe Pérez Roque, the forty-something-year-old minister of foreign affairs who had been widely viewed as a pragmatic, thoughtful Cuban politician for a younger gener-ation, along with ten other high-level government ministers and officials. "We all had to idolize them until, suddenly, they were fired, and the only reasons that we were told as to why they'd been fired were obviously fake. And *por colmo*, the 'Let-ter from Fidel' that day in *Granma* began talking about Pérez Roque and ended talking about baseball! The condescension was just . . ." She trailed off and shook her head.

Adela was alarmed that an email she'd written to a friend about a philosophy conference she'd attended on a day off had been forwarded around the community without her permission. She had complained that the Cuban intellectuals seemed to have lost the ability to debate among themselves, to be analytical and to argue. In response, she'd received emails from fellow students and academics both praising her courage for speaking up and chastising her for speaking too critically out of turn. As her frustration mounted, it was compounded by the fact that every time she tried to use the state-issued computer in her classroom to open the websites of European study grants, the screen froze. She forwarded me a flier for a study abroad expo with stops in every Latin American country but Cuba.

And she was angry that part of her job involved writing personality profiles of her *Chinitos*. Adela was asked to analyze their habits and attitudes toward authority in written reports she'd turn in at the end of the year. The task loomed as her time in Tarará drew to a close. If they were under covert surveillance, she reasoned, someone was probably writing some sort of report on her, too. That, she later told me, was why she always sent me emails rather than calling me. She was convinced that the phone was tapped, and she could more easily control what she wrote in an email than what she'd say.

/// After she spent a year at Tarará, Adela was reassigned to complete her second year of social service at an academic editorial house in Havana under a lecherous fifty-something boss who made inappropriate comments daily and had once put his hand on her leg. She could move back home to Miramar. Until that year, she told me, she had been naïve, too idealistic. It was the sort of realization that corroded her from the inside, creeping over her memories and beliefs until it seemed that she couldn't trust anything she'd thought or even been up until then.

Her grandfather had felt ill one recent morning, and she'd taken him to the hospital. They gave him an electrocardiogram and told him that he was having a bit of muscular pain; they handed the printout to Adela before she left. By that evening he was dead, she told me. Heart attack. Overcome, she asked her father, a doctor who lived on the other side of the city with his second wife, if the printout showed any signs of the attack, and he pointed out a tiny irregularity. "There." She carried the paper around with her, folded into a pocket of her wallet. Its edges wore tiny tears though she took it out carefully.

There was nothing she could do, not about her boss or about the doctors or about Raúl or Pérez Roque. "I only talk about these things when you're here," she said. She shrugged tightly and laughed. "Everyone knows all of this already. I'm the last person to learn. It's better not to talk about it. I can't do anything about anything for the next year, so why?"

Her options, as she saw them, were as follows: She could stay in Cuba, work as a professional under one of a number of aging bosses while making hardly any money, burn inside at the state of the country she loved, but live in it and remain silent to avoid consequences and wait. Or she could leave, try for a scholarship, not defect, of course, but plan to come back at some indefinite but inevitably improved future point. At least she had come to these conclusions, she said, while she still had life in front of her. What was really heartbreaking were the older people who had given up so much for something that was so obviously bankrupt. Whenever I talked to her, I had the feeling of someone stuck in a room with all the lights turned out, feeling around in the dark for a door.

She held up five fingers. "How many fingers do I have up?" she asked me. "No, there are only four fingers. See, it's like in *1984*. It doesn't matter what you say, or what reality says. Only what they say matters. *Patria o muerte: valga la redundancia.*" *Patriotism or death*, the revolutionary refrain: both mean the same thing.

/// People like Adrián worked toward art and beauty. Flashes of beauty and grace were part of what had kept Adela suspended in contentment for so many years: reading, but also wandering the halls of the national art museum, their gallery layouts known by heart, drawn to the room of Wilfredo Lam canvases to be transported by his moody Cubism. Listening to pop troubadour Carlos Varela give an impromptu concert just for students at the bottom of the university steps, the cupolas and sepia buildings of Centro Habana dominoing out behind the stage in the sagging sun. Films, and stiff wooden strips of seventy-year-old movie theater armrests biting into elbows, munching cones of popcorn or peanuts while traveling to Paris, just for a few hours at a 10 AM movie showing, or for the entire week of the French Film Festival if Adela wanted.

Beauty ran contrary to the very tangible goals of the Revolution: It served no productive end. It was the historic domain of the leisure class. It opened portholes to unknowable worlds. The expansiveness of all art was, as Reinaldo Arenas had written, a "dissident force, because a dictatorship is itself unaesthetic, grotesque; to a dictator and his agents, the attempt to create beauty is an escapist or reactionary act." But the Cuban government had colonized its country's art. After years of suppressing what didn't directly support it, the regime had mellowed into a cultural policy that promoted a vision of pluralism. This particular dictator and his agents didn't need to understand why one would create beauty to know that the cheap escapism it provided to a country hemmed in by ocean could, in fact, be productive. And this dictator had learned that creators of art could speak for the freedoms of his country more effectively than he, pinned in place as they were by privilege. Pre–Special Period cultural policy, lifted straight from the repressive Soviet Union, had ignored the propagandistic possibility of art. During the Special Period, an indecisive miasma of permissiveness and strict regulation gave rise to lugubrious films made of reels developed in Venezuela and artworks cobbled together with whatever materials could be found. Films and paintings exploded with double entendre, artists were jailed, thousands defected, and an independent art space hosted enraged political performance pieces by artists like Angel Delgado and Tania Bruguera. Delgado took a literal shit on a copy of *Granma* in the early nineties, landing him in jail for six months before he left for Mexico; Bruguera would spend much of the next decade in Chicago, though she kept a home in Havana and visited often. In interviews in which she was inevitably questioned about censorship under the Castro regime, she would nod to its existence but also point out that in the capitalist world, there was self-censorship, too, equally implicit and equally powerful, revolving around art's salability. Over the course of the next decade and a half, a system of gentle self-censorship settled into Havana's art scene. Its borders shifted and moved depending on one's chosen artistic expression—music, dance, writing, theater, visual art—and one's aversion to risk.

By the 2009 Havana Biennial, to which thousands of well-heeled international art professionals flocked, Bruguera, who had held a lecture series entitled "Art of Conduct" from 2000 to 2009 in her home in Habana Vieja to instruct young artists how to walk the fine line between censurable and prized, got an official exhibit for the artwork created through the lecture series. "I've worked on pieces that have been censored (also outside of Cuba)," Bruguera had explained in an interview in 2007, "but I thought that this one should work from inside the system to exist, because its success would not come from its censorship, but precisely from its survival (the possibility of building something)."

At gallery openings for artists whose work was just oblique enough to be mounted, I saw the occasional state security agent, the stonewashed jeans, short-sleeved button-down shirts, and cell phones in belt holsters a giveaway. They were usually too well-pressed, their clothes a fatal combination of new and out of fashion amid a well-dressed group whose casual nods to whatever trends ran through Europe or the States marked them, too. Even those who lived outside the true financial elite wore their hair the way they'd seen Spanish women do it or the H&M blouse they saved for special occasions with the long, beaded necklaces that sold for a few CUC in the artisan market downtown. Clusters of artists and art students socialized among themselves. At after-parties, we all danced to "Gozando en la Habana."

/// While Adela had been moving back to Havana, in late 2009, Adrián moved, too. He was now living in an apartment lent to him by Che Guevara's granddaughter, a freckle-faced teenager who seemed to have a crush on him. The amount of time he spent in Havana was so minimal these days, he told me, that her family let him use it if he did minor upkeep. He was still saving to buy a house, but now his daydreams set him down in a beach house at one of the *playas del este*. I saw him at a few parties where Raúl's grandkids trailed eddies of discreet whispers. He fit right in.

7

SPECIAL PERIODS

CARLOS AND ELAINE

The day that entry exam results for the Instituto Superior de Arte were posted, Carlos woke at seven, showered and dressed, and headed over to the school office ten blocks from his house in order to be there when they posted the list on the door. He was home by nine. They hadn't even put the test scores next to people's names, he said as he paced back and forth in front of Elaine and me, only pass and fail. He had no way to know how he'd done, how many answers he'd gotten right or wrong.

The only people granted spots in the film program, he said, his face sour, were the hijos de: the daughter of someone who worked at the school, the young new wife of one of Cuba's important actors, the son of a government official. He crossed his arms tight against his chest, leaving pale marks when he moved his fingers. It wasn't fair. Cool morning air wafted from the kitchen through the living room, lifting arm hairs and dispersing cigarette smoke.

The scores had been posted at eight. At eight-thirty, as he was walking home, he'd stopped to get his shells read by a *santera*. She had described Carlos's family, his goals, how he felt in that precise moment. He stood over the kitchen table, where Elaine and I sat, leaning onto his tented fingers. His knuckles were turning white and his nose pointed into the air. His voice rose with every detail and for the first time, neither Elaine nor I told him to quiet down. "Me dejó frio," he shouted, it was staggering. She had looked at him from beneath her head wrap and told him that there was nothing left for him in Cuba. He was destined to make his life elsewhere, she told him.

"I was born to do things in life," Carlos spat as he started to pace again. His eyes roamed as if hunting for the man he was certain he would become were he just given the chance. "But not here."

That he'd been denied a spot in school was vindication. He retreated into his room to disappear into the fiction of *The L Word* or *Lost* on my laptop, to nap and dream that he was elsewhere—a friend had come over with a hard drive and copied dozens of movies and TV series to my external hard drive. Carlos spent a week watching television. He emerged to eat lunch and smoke in the living room and, eventually, to go to the weekend's parties and concerts.

School had one sole objective, Carlos told me later: indoctrination, "to make you function politically like they want you to function." Propaganda, state news programs, the novels that the local publishing houses put out—they all reflected what the government deemed the best of Cuba, a country of mythic proportions and importance. I thought of Juan and Alejandra, with whom I'd become closer over long afternoons of coffee and discussion. Alejandra's eight-year-old son, who loved to draw and race me down the streets of Vedado, had come home from school on various occasions saying, "Mami, did you know that Fidel made Cuba great for the Cubans? You never told me that." Once he asked her, "Why are all Americans so bad?" And finally, recently, "Mami, why did I fail this question on a test, when the history program we watched on TV said that the answer I wrote down was correct?"

So at home, parents quietly—carefully—tried to manage expectations and lend some gray to the black-and-white world illustrated in history books and classes. Alejandra, recounting these stories to me, had widened her eyes and gripped her too-skinny wrist across the table. "Imagine. What do I tell Diego? I tell him that what he says he's learning is not true, that it's a little more complicated, and I risk his repeating it in class. What if the teacher is a real Communist and treats him poorly? What if she reports Juan and me to the CDR, tells them to keep an eye on us? Juan sells artwork without reporting it sometimes." Alejandra didn't contradict what Diego was taught until it seemed necessary. She told him that Fidel had done many things for Cuba, good and less good, that Americans were not all bad. Then she went to speak to his teacher about his grade. She wanted him to see her fighting for something that she believed was right. The teacher told Alejandra that since Diego had cited an answer that ran contrary to the government history book they'd read in school, he had failed. But what Diego wrote down was corroborated by these two sources, Alejandra argued as she flipped through other texts, and she argued all the way up to the municipal education chief, who told her that "even when the teacher is not right, in this country, the teacher is right." Diego's grade stayed the same.

And this was how Diego began to make sense of what was happening around him. Jose Martí said that to be cultured was to be free, a quote splashed about all over Cuba, and he learned about literacy rates and ballet dancers and yet he saw hypocrisy and hustling and opportunism and hunger. There were people whose actions seemed in direct contrast with not only their words but what he'd been told to expect in school. At some point, his mother wouldn't mediate these situations for him. Adolescence anywhere revolves around the recognition of a gulf between what ought to be and what is. Young Cubans were told two competing versions of what ought to be and experienced firsthand something that often clashed with both. Whether they were told how to negotiate the distance between the three inputs was variable.

This was part of the reason why Cuban kids played in the streets, not in apartments or houses. Children were like sieves that information flowed through. Kids saw things that they shouldn't: a computer that wasn't registered, as it should have been, with the Committee in Defense of the Revolution, or an unauthorized foreigner, or a delivery of eggs straight from the farmer. Kids could report an anti-Communist quip or attitude to another child's parent, which, if it bubbled all the way up, in the past had resulted in children being taken from their parents and their parents being put in reeducation camps. It rarely happened anymore, but still home was a place of vulnerability, and children threatened the tenuous peace of the Havanan ecosystems that were both sustaining and possibly deadly: From family to apartment complex to the larger community, trembling circles of trust radiated outward. Everyone had some sort of open secret to hide from the government. But the axes they all held over one another's heads stayed in the air and children remained oblivious until, at some indefinite but inevitable point of adolescence or young adulthood, they weren't.

The day Carlos didn't get into the ISA, his last hope for his place in Cuba blew apart, I thought. He'd been saving a part of himself that thought that maybe, maybe his country was changing, that left room for the fact that he could be wrong when he said that anywhere else was better than Cuba; he was self-aware enough to know that his perspective, as someone who had lived in the same apartment for his whole life, who had never been anyplace where *Granma* wasn't the newspaper and a Castro wasn't the *comandante*, was limited. He was smart enough to leave some room for the possibility that what he understood of the reality of other countries might be warped, too, and so he couldn't truly judge how Cuba stacked up against anyplace else. He had hoped, I realized as I watched him pace, that he could be canny enough to squeeze from Cuba what it could give him so that he could move into the rest of the world without regrets. His failure was complete.

Carlos's life would begin the moment he set foot outside Cuba. Anything that happened in Cuba didn't, couldn't matter. To him, goals would either disappoint him or keep him in place. If he had to be in Havana he would be there quietly, with no real attachment to anyone or anything. At the drag shows and Divino parties, he didn't seem to mind not taking men home. He dated two men while I knew him, both handsome, both romances short-lived. He wanted, one day, to replicate his parents' nuclear family, find a husband, have kids. In the promiscuous overlap of Cubans and gay men, this was who he was: the guy who never took anyone home. At parties, he and his closest friends—three men, one of whom was also named Carlos and two of whom were as tall and attractive as he—stood in a small cluster, talking shit, being present. The LGBT scene offered a sense of belonging and abstract activism, something in which Carlos could participate without the specificity that would cloud his ability to leave when the time came.

The only thing that would matter from here on out was Divino, or parties, or whatever, and the life in his mind, the life he lived when he fell asleep watching a movie until 5 AM and tricked his subconscious into believing that he was elsewhere, was real as his life in Cuba. He'd wake up in Havana again, to his mother's lunch of black beans and rice and tostones and chicken, but for those ten, twelve hours, he'd be elsewhere.

The Ballad of Elaine and Carlos was the drama of the last four decades of Cuban history played out on the tiny stage of one family's home: Elaine was a member of the last generation of adults who had been galvanized by the opportunities they'd had for education and advancement in the seventies. She'd gotten a free master's degree just because she could. Carlos was the young generation raised in the throes of economic crisis and cynicism, who struggled to see a reason why he should try. His actions were not correlated to their consequences. He could study for tests or stay out all night at parties, do not much of anything, and the only difference was that his mother yelled at him and wouldn't give him spending money. Okay, then, he could make what he'd saved from not drinking at the last few parties stretch for a few more nights.

Together they played a protracted game of the Cuban national sport, waiting, which linked hundreds of thousands of Havanans in a paralyzed stalemate. Waiting for Castro to die, waiting for something to change, waiting for visas to leave the country, ticking off days on a calendar as they passed by.

/// Fourteen percent of Cuba was over sixty in 2002. Seniors spiked to 17 percent in 2011 and the government predicted that the over-sixty set would compose a full third of the population in 2035. The government reported that the decline in birthrates owed to the high rates of university graduates nationwide, and certainly education did have some impact on the aging population—as did health care and a higher life expectancy—but what helped the rising average along were diminished numbers of Cubans of child-bearing age. So many had left in the nineties, and so many of those who stayed were loath to have children in a country they didn't trust, a country from which they hoped to depart.

A Caribbean idyll that was slowly turning gray, wrinkled, and arthritic was only the final detail of a period when real life surpassed fiction in its surrealism. During the Special Period, entire swaths of the city went without running water for years. People cut off clothing tags to patch up their shoes because the only ones for sale in Havana were made of cast plastic, and that was assuming anyone had money. Sometimes the peso pizzas they'd bought, foul six-inch-wide discs of heavy bread with sweet tomato paste, had condoms melted on top of them to look like cheese, which they plucked off before eating. Whoever couldn't afford even that survived on sugar water and bummed cigarettes. Alejandra's parents had developed X-rays for the nearby hospital on the sly, gloves on and masks over their mouths as they hunched over their bathtub. None of their friends, certainly, were allowed in for playdates. It was a two-part undertaking: Developing the film earned them a black-market paycheck, and then they brought the silty silver residue to a jeweler, who would make links out of it for a cut. They stayed up at night twisting one link around another, making chains that they could sell. Alejandra and her sister ate chicken every so often during the Special Period.

As for teenagers, "They are wavering," read a report from the massive Union of Young Communists meeting in 1992. "They simply have stopped believing or consider it impossible to resist and triumph. . . . One hears them say that everything is going wrong, that they are tired, that we have spent 30 years saying that we are in the worst moment." Young adults left. Legally and illegally, on rafts and in speedboats, via student visas, sham marriages, and lonely, compassionate foreigners. Some arrived and others did not. Everyone had a neighbor or friend whose twenty-something kid, niece, nephew, granddaughter, whoever—had just disappeared, a presumed casualty of the *balsero* crisis, when thousands of Cubans silently took to the Straits of Florida in ramshackle watercrafts made of tires and oil barrels that often fell apart mid-Straits. Sixty-year-old women cried when they talked about the Special Period.

Elaine told me about the time that she'd taken the boys with her to a social work visit in Centro Habana during the Special Period, to one of the *barbacoa* lofts constructed to divide a room vertically into two floors. They'd only known squalor à la Miramar before: Miss Havisham squalor, squalor that used to be elegance, haughty squalor. To smell shit in the street, to bat away chubby, lazy flies that had to rest on your shoulder between stops at the overflowing garbage bin and the wall, to feel the living room ceiling press on the crown of your head under the sleeping loft that three people shared and stand hungry beneath it: these tableaux inspired sentiments that Carlos and his brother hadn't yet felt.

"Shame, surprise, fear, humiliation. Because we'd thought we were equal," Carlos told me. The four of them lived in one bedroom but they never lacked food, even if it was just rice and beans, which was still among the only foods that Carlos or his brothers ate. He had never smelled the ammonia stink of a communal toilet that had to be flushed manually with buckets of water carried up flights of stairs that burned enough scant calories so that no one actually flushed it. Carlos's clothes were always clean and pressed, even if he rotated through the few shirts that he could count on one hand.

"After the Special Period, we all learned to invent," Elaine said with an exhale of smoke. "Before it, they had created a system in which we thought we deserved everything. The state was God, and it gave at will. It killed creativity, killed individuality. The Special Period woke us up."

Elaine felt a deep ambivalence about moving North. She liked her life in Havana, the visitors and the chattiness and the belonging, but Nicolas had never felt at home in Cuba, was in demeanor distinctly un-Cuban, and her sons would do better elsewhere, she sensed. Carlos did nothing, and Maykel had been driving his gypsy cab more and more, and Elaine didn't like that he hung out all night with tourists and *jineteras*. Intellectual pursuit had once been revered in Cuba, but ever since the Special Period, the way to make any kind of living was in service: serving food, doing manicures, driving cabs, renting an apartment. An improving lifestyle had been mostly severed from intellect. All she wanted were two sons who were happy, who had goals and a purpose, who lived honestly. That, she believed with the force of the rest of her life, would not happen in Havana.

Fourteen months until their visa appointment became ten months, and then eight months, and then even closer— the conversations that Elaine and I had about life in Cuba, about life in the United States, about life in Mexico and why after college I had moved there and not to New York, where I was born, or back to Oregon, where I'd grown up, grew heavier in tone.

Other foreigners had provided windows to abroad before me, a way to mediate between how the Cuban government said its country measured up to the rest of the world and what was seen on TV: Diego, a Spaniard who lived in my apartment five years ago and was now with his boyfriend downtown, and a Spanish Marxist psychologist named Angeles whom Elaine had met at a conference. Diego was Angeles's nephew, and when he'd gone to Cuba to attend a university program, they'd sent him to Elaine. Angeles and Elaine argued passionately about politics but loved each other deeply.

When Angeles came to town, Nicolas and Diego marched into the kitchen with a cooler filled with food and beer. They moved all the furniture out of the living room, because a singer friend of a friend whom Elaine had always meant to call came over and brought a mic and a speaker. Her boyfriend played background tracks on a CD player and the singer's voice bounced off the pink walls and through the stairways beyond. I bought a bottle of Havana Club at the corner store and brought over some Serrano ham to add to the stash, and we spent the day in the living room with beer and rum and a favada stew that Diego made. Neighbors popped in and out. None stayed for very long. Angeles, a woman so large it was difficult for her to climb stairs, sat at the head of the table and waved her arms as others danced, and Elaine sat next to her, between the party and her friend, her voice silked and content. Elaine and Carlos traveled by sharing.

Havana was a woman who had once been renowned for her beauty until hard times had soured her. Her hand had gotten heavy with makeup application; her necklines had crept down; her beauty was tainted with vulgarity. But sometimes, when she was alone, after she'd taken off her makeup, she danced in her garden, bare-faced and barefoot, to an old bolero, and the old elegance appeared, normal as a Tuesday evening.

8

THE REVOLUTION WILL NOT
BE TELEVISED

ENSEMBLE

Life appeared to cease when it rained in Havana. Daylight dimmed to a dark gray and humidity sealed envelopes, softened soap until it resembled sun-melted chocolate, and puckered magazines as if they'd been paged through above a steamy bathtub. Few structures were impermeable: roofs dripped, water blew in through windows that didn't close properly, and uneven floors puddled. Bus shelters were small enough that all but a few people in any crowd would be soaked by the time a vehicle arrived. Streets flooded. Sometimes teenage boys gripped back fenders and surfed behind buses in sneakers, T-shirts plastered to their chests and baggy shorts extended behind them in stiff flapping flags, their knees ominously close to wheels and their faces blazing.

Mornings felt like late afternoons, full with the sense of people in bedrooms, taking naps. Students came to class so rarely in rainstorms that instructors stopped showing up to sit before a gallery of chipped wooden chairs. Anyone caught anywhere but at home faced fresh coffee and conversation. Any event requiring elegant clothing or a prompt arrival was out of the question, postponed or cancelled implicitly, because not enough people had cars.

It was the cost, but also the government permits required to purchase one, that kept people from owning cars. Once purchased, color-coded license plates indicated in shorthand what kind of permit any given car had. For example, diplomats got black plates, the first three numbers of which specified what country the car's owner was from, and blue indicated a vehicle that belonged to the government. The rare coffee-colored plate was for a director of a Cuban company, pale green stood for the Ministry of the Interior, dark green was the Fuerzas Armadas Revolucionarias, the armed forces, and so on. Anonymous drivers were not, in fact, anonymous at all.

The armed forces had been active that winter, which Elaine knew because she had become a news junkie. Fuzzy CNN *en español* was her daily companion as she prepared the family's lunch. One morning, she charged through the door between our kitchens, calling, "Niña, ven acá." We stood in silence before her TV.

Soviet-era green planes and camouflaged bodies in formation looked ominous against the dusty earth of an undisclosed countryside location. Trenches had been dug and guns fired and Raúl Castro directed a speech toward a group of rank-and-file FAR men, his metal epaulettes glinting in the sun. These military exercises happened every few years, to stay at ready for a U.S. invasion along the lines of 1961's Bay of Pigs. It was the very end of 2009 and the four days of extensive maneuvers, strategy sessions, and military parades across the island came seven months after President Obama had lifted restrictions on Cuban American travel, remittances, and U.S. telecommunications firms looking to do business in Cuba.

"Look at the military man in his uniform, showing everyone how in control he really is," Elaine scoffed as she resumed cooking.

Another general gave a speech. "The political-military situation, which characterizes the confrontation between our country and the empire, can go from a relatively normal situation to a much more urgent, confrontational, aggressive one in a month, a week, or even in a night," said General Leonardo Andollo Valdez.

"Oh no, no, this isn't for your benefit, *hija*," Elaine said to the TV. She pointed her knife at the screen. "This is for us, just for us. To remind us exactly who's in charge."

Elaine had been barbed and bitter since Maykel had been called to complete his year of military service, compulsory for all Cuban men. He wouldn't be allowed to apply for an exit visa without finishing it. He had a new girlfriend, a ballerina, and was making good money with the car and had hinted at staying. The weather had been rainy and cool lately, odd for late autumn. And Carlos, she learned, was now too old to apply for a visa as a dependent. Elaine and Nicolas would leave their sons behind and file for family reunification visas in the States. The Reyes family wouldn't emigrate to Miami together, after all; if the four of them made it, it would be separately.

/// The military exercises were happening for a reason, one that neither the Reyes family nor I knew about at the time. Tiny bursts of protest were erupting across Havana.

In October 2009, an argument at the art university had turned into a cafeteria protest over the foul food that students—many of whom were dancers—were given at the *becas.* "I'm not going to class," shouted a student surrounded by a circle of about a hundred nodding people. On the video that was uploaded to the Internet, he is filmed from the back in a yellow T-shirt and a blue baseball cap. His watch glints in the sun as he waves his arms. "This isn't a demonstration, we're not going on a strike . . . we're just trying to *resolver* the problems that are affecting us, like our health, because most of the kids in this program are sick or getting sick," he says, directing his comments at two older men who stand at the front of the circle, their arms crossed in front of their chests. They shake their heads.

The student holds up a tray of gray food: gluey mash over rice, watery beans, a sugared lump of dessert. "I've been here for five years, I'm in my final year, and I can't remember the last time I saw a piece of pork or a decent piece of chicken on this plate," he hollers over hoots of support. Castro and the generals never eat like this, he continues; they ride in cars and wear jewelry and eat meat.

He climbs onto a chair or a bench, his head and shoulders above the crowd now, and he talks through the lack of freedom of expression and censorship in Cuba. "We need to be united!" he shouts. "If they ask me, I'll say what I think. You should, too." Students yell and clap.

Another video was released a few days later. The same student stands alone in a room, now, and reads from a sheet of paper." To our leaders, listen to the voices of your students. We are the young people in whom has been planted the essence of the Revolution . . . we will give our blood and sweat to this Revolution . . . but our great love is art. . . . It's not logical to take measures that are both difficult and questionable, like the lack of proper hygienic conditions, the awful quality of food, and the unacceptable amount that is offered . . . it would be inappropriate for a young revolutionary like me to accept a reality like this."

After a two-minute speech, it cuts to a newscaster, who explains that these comments are a follow-up to some discontent voiced at "el ISA." That first time, the clean-cut, gray-haired newscaster says, the student had spoken "with no papers." He looks like he is trying to hide a smile, as if he either agrees with the young man or finds the situation risible. He cuts to a clip of the protest: "We don't have freedom to say things . . . don't ask my opinion if you don't want to hear it," the student had shouted.

"Within the Revolution, everything; against the Revolution, nothing." This was the policy upon which Fidel had settled in 1961, after a purge of an overly critical intellectual scene that writer Guillermo Cabrera Infante called "Kafka in Cuba, Prague in Havana."

Just after the Revolution, Cabrera Infante, the son of founders of the Cuban Communist Party and the editor of *Revolución*'s newsmagazine, *Lunes de Revolución*, had in two and a half years expanded the periodical from six pages to sixty-four, and one hundred thousand copies to a quarter million. After a documentary about Havana's nightlife made by the other Cabrera Infante brother was banned by the Party-run film commission in 1961, *Lunes* collected signatures in protest and its staff were subsequently called in for a meeting with Castro, Che, Haydée Santamaría, Armando Hart—the minister of education and soon-to-be minister of culture—and others. All involved intellectuals, "and then some," Cabrera Infante later wrote, were invited.

Fidel Castro himself talked to us. Characteristically, he had the last word. Getting rid first of the ever-present Browning 9mm fastened to his belt—making true a metaphor by Goebbels: "Every time I hear the word culture, I reach for my pistol"—Castro delivered one of his most famous speeches, famous not for being eight hours long, but for being brief and to the point for the first time since he became Cuba's Prime Minister," wrote Cabrera Infante. His deposition is now called "Words to the Intellectuals" and it ends with a résumé which Castroites everywhere claim to be a model of revolutionary rhetoric but which is really a Stalinist credo: "Within the Revolution, everything," he thundered like a thousand Zeuses. "Against the Revolution, nothing!"

The result of the meeting, apart from Castro's speech: The film was still banned and the newsmagazine closed, owing to "an acute shortage of newsprint." Eventually, *Revolución* was reborn as *Granma*. Cabrera Infante left Cuba in 1965 and died in 2005 in England, where he had lived since, publishing novels and political essays that questioned the validity of a system that taught its citizens to read but controlled what was published.

These were the sorts of questions that had been posed to the then-president of the National Assembly a year earlier at the University of Information Sciences. Computer programming students had passed around a microphone at what had been billed as a speech by Ricardo Alarcón, broadcast to all of the school's 10,000 students on closed-circuit television. One student in particular had aired eloquent complaints about the regime and its inconsistencies, spurring cheers of the same tone as those that had wafted through the ISA. But in this case, the confrontation had been quickly covered in the Spanish press under a headline adapted from a student's quote: "If only we could travel and see the real world."

To that statement, Alarcón had infamously responded that, if the globe's "six billion inhabitants could travel wherever they wanted, the collisions that there would be in the world's air would be enormous." The quote was prominent in the news articles. And within days, the students appeared on national television and Cubadebate.com, the Communist

Party's YouTube channel, slumped in a semicircle of plastic chairs. Any criticism was meant to be taken constructively as ways to improve the Revolution, "to better construct socialism, and not to destroy it." The foreign media, they said, had perverted their intent. This was what the capitalist media did, blew things out of proportion and imposed its own agenda on independent actions. They were good kids, students, not political dissidents. Of course they'd meant to act within the Revolution.

Some dissidents meant to act against whatever it was that the Revolution meant today. Blogger Yoani Sánchez was defined by an antirevolutionary stance carved from blog posts that focused on the indignities of everyday life for Cubans under the Castros. Her emphatic writing was translated into sixteen languages and had earned her a spot in *Time* magazine's 2008 Most Influential People issue. Yet few Cubans in Havana knew who she was until early that November, when she reported that she was tossed in an unmarked black car by two plainclothes officers from the Ministry of the Interior. She emerged, she wrote, battered and bruised. When foreign reporters pressed her, a few days after the incident, to show the marks that officers had left on her body, she demurred: the only bruises that remained, she said, were on her buttocks. Three weeks later, her husband, also a blogger and dissident, was heckled and then beaten by a pro-government mob. MinInt officers had thrown him into a car, too, but this time to remove him to safety. "Did you hear about that Internet writer, *whatshername*," replaced the previous electoral year's optimism in living room conversations among the politically engaged.

The United States government wanted to support this sort of dissent. In 2008, $45 million had been dispersed to nongovernmental organizations focused on promoting democracy in Cuba via the U.S. Agency for International Development. But because the Cuban government existed to crush dissent in reality, with physical actions rather than Internet smear campaigns, many American plots appeared absurd, as if they'd been sketched out by *Our Man In Havana*'s Wormold himself. Two of the initiatives supported by U.S. taxpayers included Radio Martí, a radio station that broadcast Miami programming toward Cuba but was blocked on all Cuban radios by the state, and a plan to smuggle satellite equipment into the country disguised as boogie boards. This last scheme was discovered by Cuban informants in the States before implementation and never came to fruition. These actions went largely unknown by Cubans in Cuba. What was known, was splashed across *Granma* in angry black-and-red headlines, was declaimed on the *Mesa Redonda* nightly news program, was called neocolonial espionage, was that some dissidents were in fact on the U.S. payroll. When this turned out to be true—about 4 percent of U.S. pro-democracy funding was spent on the ground, supporting dissidents, I learned—I was surprised.

Even when reimbursed by the Americans, dissent, acting outside the Revolution, appeared to have little purpose. Nothing linked one event to another in Havana, though from the outside, there seemed to be a clear connection: school protests, military exercises, dissident beatings, and, that winter, a jailed American. The American was arrested in Cuba in December 2009 while working on a secretive USAID-contracted program.

In the absence of any independent local media or a unified response to the events, the narrative of protest had no visible arc or discernible crescendo. Television had allowed Castro, in 1960, when there were more TVs in Cuba than in Italy, to create a common enemy in the personage of "counterrevolutionaries," to link disparate events in a story of his regime's success, to spread propaganda with an illusion of candor, to create the illusion of a consensus and punish those, like the staff at *Lunes de Revolución*, who would have punctured it. State news programs now showed contrite protesters but not the protests themselves, skipping straight past the meetings and the consequences to the repentance and forgiveness.

The TV showed military exercises and Union of Young Communist parades like the one I stumbled into that winter. Students walked down the hill from the university into Centro Habana with headphones in their ears, girls linked arm in arm and gossiping, boys positioning themselves strategically to bump into the girls they'd been checking out. Brassy rhythms floated from speakers. Photographers from foreign news outlets crouched at waist-level on the edges of the street. Cameras rolled for Cuban state television. Traffic was stopped in all directions.

/// That winter was the coldest to visit Havana in years. A few warm days tucked into January weeks with temperatures that dropped as low as 38 degrees Fahrenheit. Havana is not made for true winter, a fact clarified by the deaths of between twenty-six and fifty-four adults in the state-run psychiatric hospital, depending on who was to be believed—the Cuban media or dissident activists. The hospital, known as La Mazorra for the estate on which it had been built, reportedly starved its patients, too. The accusation, seemingly borne out by grim photos of bony yellow corpses, was a gesture back in time to 1898, when four hundred Mazorra patients died of starvation between January 1 and February 27.

Elaine, Nicolas, and their sons had spent those days bundled in every long-sleeved shirt and sweater they owned, multiple pairs of socks on all eight family feet. They cuddled under the covers on Elaine and Nicolas's bed to watch movies on their new Chinese laptop, night bleeding into day and then back into night, accompanied through this weather crisis by characters from *Lost*, a show about people stuck on an island with season upon season of metaphysical explanations as to why.

Then, in February, political dissident Orlando Zapata Tamayo died after eighty-five days on a hunger strike. After six years in jail on charges of "disrespect," "public disorder," and "resistance," he'd stopped eating and died, a husk of a body. People alternately praised Zapata's *cojones* and scoffed that the truly tragic part of his story was that he actually believed that his death could have an impact. *Granma* announced that Zapata had been a sad casualty of the war with the United States, pushed toward his death by the forces of imperialism.

"Look at him," a friend of Carlos said to me. It was a few nights after Zapata's death and we walked to a party in the dark, damp night. "That man had nothing to lose. They filmed his family in their shack of a house, and *m'ija*, it was bad. He was poor, black, and definitely not one of *them*."

As much as she disagreed with the regime—and she definitely did, she said, it was indefensible at this point, fifty years of the same family!—her parents had managed to eke out some sort of privilege in Havana. They had a nice house, even if it was in a far-off suburb; her stepdad had a subterranean construction business that the administration tacitly blessed by allowing it to grow; she was studying her first-choice career, journalism. Hypocrisy had long since become a way of life, she said. She had been active in the Union of Young Communists for a while, even. Besides, the regime wasn't quite indefensible—the health-care system was still a success. Even Guillermo Fariñas, one of four men who had also declared hunger strikes after Zapata's death, was in a hospital on intravenous support right now.

Another friend jumped into the debate; the three of us now walked at the head of a column of ten people scattered down the center of Vedado streets. That posture was exactly what ensured that eventually things would change. Everyone under the age of, say, forty, even the people who were in the UJC, even the people who had done what was necessary and kissed the asses in front of them to get power in Cuba, they knew what had to happen to pull the country out of the dire situation it had been stuck in ever since the U.S.S.R. had crumpled. They'd wait until the generals died off and then they'd slowly start introducing changes.

"But that could take years and years and years," I exclaimed. "Every one of us here could have UJC-aged kids by the time that happens."

"I never said it would be short-term."

The journalist nodded. Even her revolutionary aunt, who had been someone in politics, who had loved the Revolution enough to donate a collection of valuable René Portocarrero paintings to the country and then seen only the minor ones in the museum, because the major paintings hung over the mantles of generals—even her Communist aunt said she respected the dissident, dying in protest of his captivity as a common criminal.

They wouldn't eat, the hunger strikers said, until the government recognized them as what they were: prisoners of conscience. They were traitors, spat state media. They, like the other fifty-eight dissidents in jail, were independent journalists or librarians, all men, most detained in accordance with one of three legal articles that penalized "dangerousness" or cooperation with the U.S. government. The hunger strikers were two or three people who had been sadly manipulated by capitalist forces, by agents like that American in prison. They were trying to hijack history, and the fact was, the majority of the people of Cuba were not in agreement with them. After all, it had been government agents who had pulled that dissident blogger away from the citizens who were driven to violence by his lies.

But this wasn't what we discussed in the Reyes kitchen. What we did discuss was the agriculture congress. A quarter-million small farmers and private co-op owners had just met with the Cuban vice president to discuss production short-falls. Initial government claims that it was the international economic crisis and the U.S. embargo that stunted the agri-cultural sector's growth were scoffed away. Conversation had, by all accounts, been frank; increased privatization of the industry was necessary to speed progress. Such measures were devised. "The bureaucracy holds back the production of pork in the capital," agreed a *Granma* headline a few days later. Rather than focusing on linguistic abstractions, reform-ist zeal would be better used to push for something with tan-gible consequences for all. Verbiage was negotiable when it came to pork or lettuce—but not politics.

/// It's easy to forget in the winter, when the shadows of buildings harbor cool air and it's warm but crisp in the sun, just how hot Havana gets in the summer. And then summer begins in April and you resent the air for not being water and think only thirsty amphibious thoughts until you are either in water or drinking water beneath a fan.

There were good reasons why I hadn't seen Sandra in a while: The rains made the trip to San Miguel del Padrón cumbersome and expensive; she had run out of phone min-utes and didn't call back when I left messages at her aunt's— too busy, said the aunt, with baby Mia; I was interviewing other people and pretended that I didn't wonder constantly how she, Aboo, and Mia were. One afternoon I set out for

San Miguel uninvited, bringing a Christmas gift that I'd forgotten to give her the last time I saw her, a sparkly wallet someone had given me that I knew I'd never use. I envisioned it poking out of her black faux–patent leather purse. My *máquina* dropped me at the main road and I headed straight for a convenience store cabin, small CUC dispensaries open only through chest-high eight-inch horizontal slits through which the attendant passed whatever goods had been purchased. I stood on the street to buy a bottle of cold water and bent my head down low to feel the air conditioning. The lines were long for the Frozzen machines, though the watery soft-serve started to melt into its airy crunchy cone as soon as its buyer walked down the street. I walked slowly to Sandra's.

A woman in legging jeans and an orange halter top that stopped three inches above her bellybutton waltzed toward me, equidistant from each sidewalk, framed by the skimpy palm trees. Her breasts looked tenuously contained. Six-inch silver heels with Lucite platforms pushed her hips out and to the side in dramatic sways and her shoulders followed.

"Hooooolia!" Sandra exclaimed as we drew closer. "What are you doing here?"

"To see you," I responded quickly, and just as quickly, she turned around, wrapped her hand around my elbow, and guided me toward her house.

"You've got to see how much the baby's grown. I was just going to get Yessica to head downtown but you've got to see the baby first."

The baby, whose fuzzy cap of black hair thoroughly covered her head and ears, was no longer a baby but moving toward toddler-hood. As we sat in the living room, Yessica peeked her head in. They were heading to Vedado first to see about anyone on Paseo and *malecón*, and if there were no quick takers, they'd go to a club in Miramar. I could join if I paid for taxis and their cover charges. They'd negotiate the prices down.

But we had to stop by the Sylvain bakery first, so Sandra could tell Gallego something. He was working one day on, two days off there now, because there weren't enough jobs to go around and so he split shifts with another neighborhood man. Yessica banged on the door six times as Sandra cupped her hands around her mouth and shouted. After a minute or two, the door cracked, and a tall, muscular, black man with the rotund belly of someone much shorter and fatter grumped out, "What do you want?" as he turned toward the door. Sandra leaned against the doorjamb and raised her eyebrows. Instantly, he tossed open the door, walked toward the back, and shouted over his shoulders that everyone was *en llamas* because they'd gotten no oil and so they were baking bread licked with water rather than its usual brushing of oil or butter and everything was sticking but they had to make quota so they'd be working late. I walked toward the cavernous production room imagining the machines that must once have sat in front of the now-empty ovens that lined the hall, toward the group of six men in sleeveless white uniforms who slapped dough onto baking sheets. They stopped just long enough to look Sandra and Yessica over while Sandra told Gallego to be sure to bring home what he was supposed to bring home. Then Sandra turned around and we left. He had, she told me, gotten bad about bringing back the portion of breadsticks that, like the salary, he split with the neighbor. She had to remind him. She did everything in that house.

A cursory stop at the *malecón* was followed by a *máquina* to Miramar. At the club, we ordered beers, began to drink and sway in our chairs to the music. After a second round, Sandra said that we should go downstairs to buy more

Bucaneros—they were cheaper. We could stuff them into my large canvas tote bag and pour them into our glasses upstairs, and the waitresses wouldn't even notice. Downstairs, when the bartender's back was turned toward the coolers, Sandra reached her long, pink nails into the shot glass of toothpicks on the bar and slid them into my bag, and then asked for extra paper napkins, which followed the toothpicks. That night she spirited out all six of the accompanying beer glasses for the six beers we ordered upstairs. Three for each Sandra and Yessica, glasses that they wouldn't have to buy at *la chopin.*

A man across the room, separated from us by three small aluminum bistro tables, had been eyeing Yessica. At a slower song, Sandra stood and walked over to him, sashayed, really. Since she'd stopped breastfeeding, her body had returned more or less to normal, though her stomach was looser and striated. Leaning over his shoulder not quite close enough to touch, she told him about Yessica. He couldn't handle her, Sandra murmured, he'd do better not to hook up with her in the first place because he wouldn't even know what to do with her, she was so crazy and hot in bed, he'd never be satisfied with anyone else. Yessica sat silently, pulling her shoulder-length brown hair back and forth along her lips, hiding her face. She wore white capris and a purple ruffled tank top. The man's eyes were an evolution of curious to hungry to questioning to skeptical and, as Sandra walked away, disdainful as he turned to his friends and laughed. Sandra shrugged. He was replaceable. She'd work on her salesmanship. It was easier to be convincing when she was talking about herself.

Nothing startled Sandra. She never let on to fear or admitted agitation: not over the cold (she and Mia, Aboo, and Gallego had turned on their gas burner for heat and huddled) or poverty ("I've done without") or Cuba or the world abroad or men. Every situation could be solved. She escaped the police when they'd come after her for using the Spanish ex-fiancée's ATM card to withdraw a few hundred CUC after— she tossed the card and paid a hospital attendant $30 to admit her, claiming that she hadn't answered his calls because she'd been sick and the card was obviously not on her person. She did not entertain what-ifs. "Anyone who's scared should get a dog," she told me when I next saw her a few weeks later.

But there were stories, she continued. . . . We walked, now, to the cafeteria near her place for *cafecitos*. Aboo watched Mia. There were stories, Sandra said, of girls from San Miguel who'd gotten into trouble. There was the girl who was offered $500 to eat shit, literally, a fetish that Sandra wouldn't have humored, but this girl did it and went straight to the hospital afterward. She died within a few days of an infection. There was the girl whose Italian boyfriend had swept her off to Europe and sent her to an optometrist to have a small wart on her eyelid removed. The surgeon was really a black-market organ rustler, and the girl was sent back to Cuba without eyeballs—the boyfriend had a blind daughter and all he wanted was the girl's eyes. There was the neighbor who married a man from "one of those crazy Arab countries," Sandra said, "where women are things and sign away their rights when they get married." He abused her, and she wanted to leave him but couldn't. He eventually traded her for a camel to another man—traded for a camel! The last straw, the straw after the last straw. She escaped, said Sandra, ran across the desert dying of thirst to the Cuban embassy. Now she's back in San Miguel. But of course none of what Sandra said could be verified.

Here are the facts, culled from independent newspaper articles, in the case of the April 2010 death of Roberto Baudrand: He was the Chilean manager of the joint-venture firm Alimentos Rio Zaza, which produced milk, fruit juices, wines, and other foods in Cuba, and whose annual profits of approximately $9 million were split equally between the Cuban government and a Chilean businessman named Max Marambio. Before his business career, Marambio had been a guard for the only Marxist president of Chile, Salvador Allende, and when Allende committed suicide after a military coup ousted him in 1973, Marambio went to Cuba to perform elite clandestine missions as a top-level spy. Whether Marambio was in fact a close friend of Fidel Castro was uncertain. The Cuban government had frozen $23 million of funds associated with Alimentos Rio Zaza in association with a corruption investigation. Baudrand had been informed two weeks before his death that he would not be allowed to leave the country until further notice. He had not been kept in police custody, but he had been brought in various times for questioning.

Baudrand, fifty-nine, had been retained in Raúl Castro's effort to root out corruption at the highest levels of government and business. Corruption, wrote economist Esteban Morales in Cuban state media, was the real counterrevolution. "It's becoming evident that there are people in government . . . who are entrenching themselves financially for the time when the revolution falls," he wrote, and those people were more dangerous to the Cuban Revolution than political dissidents.

Here was what the foreign press printed as "possibly" and "maybes": Baudrand had been retained in association with an ongoing scandal that involved Cubana Airlines. An autopsy by Cuba's Institute of Legal Medicine found that he'd died of "acute respiratory insufficiency" caused by drugs and alcohol. Maybe it had been a suicide or an overdose. Or, as his family said they had been told, he'd died of a heart attack.

Baudrand had people at the airport, everyone whispered: The "corruption scandal" was really a scheme in which

Cubans bankrolled by family abroad would arrive at the airport with nothing and slip aboard flights to Uruguay and Chile and Argentina, filling empty seats. Baudrand paid off enough people between takeoff and landing that his clients would—without papers, without passports—get out of the country on planes that, once grounded in any other country, would mean freedom. No way had he committed suicide, people scoffed, or died of heart failure.

Rio Zaza stopped producing milk, wine, *Ron Planchao*, and fruit juice. The practical application of this news, and the rumors, was the reality that the only place to buy any milk other than the powdered sort was Palco, the far-off grocery store frequented by diplomats, which sold passionfruit gelato, imported frozen apricots, and $100 bottles of wine. Palco, which cost me $6 to get to in a taxi after some negotiation with the driver, carried a long-life German brand of milk, but only on the days when they'd recently gotten a shipment. Expat housewives bought the Tetra Pak milk in cases for their small children. I bought six at a time.

Rumor was what united individual stories, pulled them together into arcs with consequences that could be understood by evidence snatched from daily life. And so there was a gulf between what Cubans lived through and what the international media said was happening in Havana. By the time news of any sort made its way through the community, it felt disconnected, diluted, as if it had happened three days earlier and somewhere else. People were still getting deliveries of black-market yogurt and hot dogs and trying their best to make ends meet and not stand out. There had been a food shortage, yes, but new regulations for farmers were helping to increase production and privatization. What impact could that march/beating/death/protest/military exercise have on daily life?

/// Stay inside, the bed beckoned during a storm, whether you are alone or accompanied. It's not worth leaving, whispered each raindrop as it descended. So I learned to do what Lucía and Elaine and everyone else did. I opened the window to let the sounds gush in and every time it rained I stayed home. Besides, these worlds opened by movie and book and bed all dulled the impulse to speculate on what couldn't be known. Finite spaces, an imagined reality drawn by someone else, or an interpersonal drama were a relief.

Fernando Pérez's biopic of nineteenth-century Cuban intellectual and revolutionary José Martí—officially known as the "Apostle of Freedom"—came out that winter. Havana's international airport and national library are named after him, and his likeness stares down upon the Plaza de la Revolución, the José Martí Anti-Imperialist Platform in front of the U.S. Interests section, and the Parque Central and the old men who talk baseball on its benches. A white bust of Martí sits outside every single school in Cuba, large or small.

Theaters usually showed pirated American films—*Avatar* had shown on state TV in Cuba while it was still in theaters in the United States—and the crowd at a Clive Owen action film from 2005 was usually only slightly different from that for an Andrei Tarkovsky film at the Cine Acapulco. *Martí*, though, played at theaters for the better part of two months.

Martí, among the leaders of the first struggles for independence from Spain, was impetuously claimed as champion on both sides of the Straits: He had both insisted on freedom from an imperial force and advocated for democracy. The two sides vaunted different aspects of his philosophy to explain how his vision of Cuba's future was correct. After 1959, when economic mechanisms of control were severed, Cuba was finally freed from the rule of both the Spanish and the Americans, as he had said it must be; or Cuba was still struggling toward freedom, is still not the democracy that Martí envisioned.

The film focused not on his days as a journalist and exile from Spanish Cuba in New York, or his popular writings, or his death in battle with the Spaniards in 1895 at age forty-two, which had sparked anti-Spanish sentiment into action. This film focused instead on his youth. Martí grew up as the son of middle-class Havana Spaniards and went to school with other children of privilege. In the film, their parents are loyal to the throne, but "Pepe" Martí and his peers begin to suspect that some sort of justice is being evaded in the system they're ordered to respect. In one scene, a teacher—a bearded, graying, lisping Spaniard—asks them what democracy means, thinking he will elicit a response typical of high-class boys. It is, after all, the 1860s.

One of the boys shouts that in Cuba there is neither freedom of expression nor freedom of the press, both of which are essential elements of a society in which the people rule themselves. An argument erupts over what it means to be a democratic state, why it is important, and how Cuba has never known democracy. The teacher raises his hands in the air as if to tamp down what he's loosed. His eyes are wild, helpless. Pepe climbs atop a schoolroom chair and says that Cubans must rule themselves. The people will not be satisfied until they see themselves represented in the institutions that rule them. The film rolled on.

On emerging from the dark theater with seats that smelled of the previous day's rain into the bright street and scent of leaded gasoline, the bustle outside made me wonder if I'd imagined the scene. Perhaps I was reading too much into it, egged on by the events of a dramatic winter. This was a film that was playing in most of Havana's theaters and had been for months.

The rest of the film had been elegiac, calm, with a camera that clung to raindrops dripping from the enormous leaves of plants, a setting in the fecund countryside, costumed militiamen that looked nothing like what Raúl's troops wore today. Horses pushed carts through streets; there were no Chevys or tanks. The actor that played Martí was distinctly not discussing Castro. But these were the conversations that were had in dining rooms, on patios, in quiet moments among people who trusted one another. The electric, pointed scene became, to me, a collective secret sitting hard and cold in the chest, yet another piece of evidence that change was a when, not an if.

This parallel was Pérez's intent. "Martí lived through things that young Cubans here could be living through also," he told me when I interviewed him for a magazine a year later. "So one has to wonder; what would I do? What Martí did, or no? They're the same issues: freedom of the press, concept of democracy, or the lack of freedom of the press so that no one participates—I see a series of situations that are conflicts for a young person. That had to be in the movie. I wanted a young audience to establish that association."

If the association was made, it was kept quietly. There were a few key differences between Martí's era and today's. Martí had been sentenced to six years in prison at age sixteen for an unsent letter in which he accused a friend who had enlisted in the Spanish army of being a traitor. The student who had led the ISA protest that autumn had simply been asked to shift his words around and show up on state TV. Jail was tangible in the same way that bad cafeteria food or farmers without seeds were tangible. Lack of freedom of expression and the press, wearing hypocrisy for a moment in order to protect your family, were abstractions.

Standing on a chair to shout about woes required innocence: a faith that someone was listening, a belief that the ten, twenty, fifty rapt faces around the chair could multiply, a specific ratio of recklessness to yearning. The young people who'd been protesting in 2009 and 2010 innocently believed that the small pieces of evidence they'd found were enough to link daily life to abstraction in a way that might create a narrative of change. This was what protected them. Food could be addressed and abstractions could be twisted. And so young people who loved their country and wanted to improve it were taught, in the quiet rebuffing of their efforts to push toward change, that if they wanted to participate more than obliquely in the creation of a national narrative, they would be invited to leave. Guillermo Fariñas and other hunger strikers were eventually given exit visas.

Everyone—Martí, Elaine, farmers, Sandra, dissidents—wanted the same thing, the same thing I wanted. They wanted some sense of control over their own futures. In Cuba, you were free to choose your fate until it bumped into the country's fate. Then you were invited to make your destiny elsewhere.

/// Five days before Lucía was to leave definitively for Chile—seven days before her entry visa expired—an earthquake shook the country from the Andes to the sea. It was the sixth-largest earthquake ever recorded on a seismograph. Carlos, still awake at six in the morning, had seen the news on CNN. He called Lucía in Ciego de Ávila, where she'd spent her final two weeks after giving up her apartment in Havana, to give her the news. "I don't know whether to scream from frustration or shout with joy," she told me the next day. She had been tepid about leaving, which everyone said was the normal response during the weeks leading up to departure: Everyone repented the ambition that had driven the desire to leave. Faced with the reality of saying good-bye to everything she'd known for a future she couldn't imagine, unsure that she'd ever return, and enjoying the weeks of farewell parties that eclipsed the memory of everyday life, Lucía questioned her decision. An undercurrent of anticipation and air of tragedy added up to the expectation of action but no action itself.

Starting a new life in a country dealing with a natural disaster wasn't ideal, so Lucía decided to wait. There was no way she'd get a job in Chile in the next month, she said, and she didn't have the money to support herself without one for long. The Chileans gave her a six-month visa extension and the airline charged her a $75 change fee for an open-ended ticket. She could borrow money from a friend and her landlady hadn't yet found another tenant. She'd leave soon, she said, after things settled down and the Chilean economy began to recover.

9

LEAVERS

LUCÍA

"Did you hear? Claudio left."

"Left where? How?"

"His brother sent for him. His brother in Miami. Sent a boat. *Se fue pa la yuma.*"

Claudio, Lucía's upstairs neighbor, had never talked about leaving. He talked about everything else—on an island of fast-talkers, Claudio was fastest. He was smallish and wiry, his voice nasal, his eyes buggy, and at age twenty-six, his brown hair was already thinning into a widow's peak. Claudio had quit school at fifteen to lie on a bare mattress in a spare room at his grandmother's apartment, three floors up from Lucía's, train the fan on himself, and read. His favorites were William Faulkner and John Dos Passos. He hated Hemingway: "so macho, no feeling, only something you Americans, who lack machismo in daily life, could like." Classic books were cheap in Cuba, where they were reprinted by the state without fear of lawsuits and sold for next to nothing. After blowing through his grandmother's library, Claudio read art and architecture history texts and took himself on midnight rambles. He knew which decrepit building in Old Havana had a running fountain in its courtyard and neighbors who didn't care if he sat alongside it into the early hours of the morning. He'd led me, one night when we left a party downtown at the same time and I was living in Centro Habana, on a tour of the neighborhood's darkest streets. Here, he gestured, was the only known exemplar of Paris-style art nouveau in Havana: Those spikes up at the top of the building were used, when debutantes in fluffy gowns had idled in the neighborhood's sitting rooms in the early twentieth century, to hoist baby grands up from the street and through the French doors of a third-floor living room. We wandered for an hour and when I finally told him I was tired, a manic energy in his eyes snuffed out. Claudio craved an audience.

When he got going, Claudio connected hot dogs and symbolism and patriotism, or Meyer Lansky and state-mandated curfews and policemen who checked *carnets*, reeling paragraphs that left the Cubans in the group nodding and slapping their knees and me cartwheeling behind him, wondering if I'd understood correctly. He was the most intellectually sophisticated person I knew in Havana, though he'd never eaten at a restaurant and he didn't own a TV.

Claudio had only begun to work the month before I heard that he'd left town. With no high school degree, no party affiliation, and no military service, the only job he could get was as a janitor. But thanks to a friend of Lucía's, Claudio was a janitor at the National Union of Cuban Writers and Artists. At least he was surrounded by like-minded people, he had told me one afternoon as he pulled old film stills of Cuban actors from the sixties out of a manila folder he'd found in the bottom of an abandoned filing cabinet. He thrust them in front of me. Someday, he was sure, someone would recognize what he was.

Then one day his mother called him with the news that his brother had sent for them. The brother had paid someone in Miami to ferry them north in a good speedboat that could carry a few dozen people. Claudio and his mother would arrive on American soil and be granted residency under the "wet foot, dry foot" policy. So they went to one of the provinces where the coastline wasn't as heavily guarded and huddled in two rooms for five days with the forty-three people who'd be their shipmates. Twenty men, nine children, and the rest women. But word got out, the house was raided, and they were put in jail for twenty-four hours. They were released and headed back to Havana. This happened three times in four weeks: a train out east, a few days' holding pattern, waiting for the sign that the bought-off border guy was on duty. Guards, tides, coast guard all had to line up right. The other times they weren't arrested, but the timing hadn't been opportune. Claudio told me the story on the phone, trying to get hold of Carlos. He'd decided to stay down there, not far from Lucía's hometown of Ciego de Ávila, and wait for the next attempt locally. He had not, in fact, left.

Lucía had spent much of her time in Ciego since early in the winter. It wasn't that her parents didn't understand why she wanted to leave; everyone knew why young people, especially young professionals, wanted to leave Cuba. But Lucía's imminent departure had been such a source of stress for her mother that her vitiligo, the skin condition that the sixty-year-old thought she'd beaten—Cuban doctors had developed an effective treatment—had returned. Lucía didn't want to feel guilty, but it crept up on her anyway, slithering through the days she'd hoped to keep spending enjoying Havana. Though she'd moved back into her apartment, into the twin bed surrounded by milk-crate nightstands piled now with fewer books since she'd given most away, she would relocate to Ciego for two weeks of nearly each month until she rescheduled her flight.

Lucía was waiting not, I thought, for economic stability in Chile, but for a sign. She wanted some assurance that she was making the right decision, some sense of what awaited her. Her group of friends had been slowly thinning, and she knew it would continue, but none of those who'd departed had come back to visit and spread stories of their first few months gone. As her peers continued to leave, she'd begun, in her last year in Cuba, to run with a group she referred to as *los adolescentes. Los adolescentes* were the throbbing heart of every party, standing in circles and pulsating: jumping up and down if excited, dancing as if they were trying to get to heaven. They talked fast and laughed faster and they wore trendy clothes, last season's Old Navy polo shirts for the boys, sent out by cousins in Miami, and stacked bangle bracelets for the girls. They came from good families and were studying what they wanted to study: graphic design and sociology and art. They walked to class jauntily, greeting the same old woman who'd sold them morning coffee every day since they began. On the days they got their student stipends from the government, which they knew weren't enough to help their families, they bought *cangrejos*, croissant-like rolled pastries, at the kiosk after class, or they traded their pesos for CUC and bought a bottle of red Vino Nazareño for $5 or they went to Turf on a Thursday. Later, when someone's aunt had left her Habana Vieja apartment to be looked after while on a trip, they pooled money for Habana Club rum and someone brought a boom box and, under lights that anywhere else would have dissuaded dancing, they talked shit and danced and grew slowly drunk.

Four would pass out on the queen mattress in the bedroom, another two on the hard sofa in the living room, and as the sun rose clear and sharp in the broken, picturesque streets, shining off the water in the gutters from the women who'd already mopped their front parlors, they'd sit on a corner, waiting for a bus that'd take them back home to unsurprised and unworried parents in Vedado or La Lisa.

Lucía had been an *adolescente* once, though she'd lived in the *beca* for students from the countryside. She knew acutely what she was leaving behind: homeland, a source of income, friends she loved, concerts and film festivals where she knew people and could talk her way into the after-party, her family. She didn't work that hard and had enough for rum and cover charges and second-hand clothes, the boyfriend jeans she'd just bought at the peso shop to wear with the pumps that her father, who made leather goods he sold at a Cayo Coco resort, had designed for her based on shoes in a foreign fashion magazine a Canadian photographer had left behind. But her choice was either to leave or be left. Someday, when Lucía was a little older, twenty-year-old friends would feel more foolish than companionable. This—the knowledge that she'd be pressed down into ever-younger social groups, back into a phase of life she'd already left, or be largely alone—was the only assurance she would get.

So Lucía spent time in Ciego, trying to remind herself that she had a game plan and it might get worse before it got better, but it was under way. If I came to visit her, we'd have to share her brother's downstairs room, she told me on the phone one afternoon, as she'd done for her entire childhood. He'd just gotten his girlfriend pregnant and was building an addition to the house, a second-floor apartment in which his new family would live. There was dust everywhere, but we could get to Cayo Coco in one of the employee buses that brought out tour guides like her brother and lounge for a day on one of the most beautiful beaches in the Caribbean for an 8-CUC day pass. She'd been only once before, to visit a ballerina friend who'd vacationed for a week at an all-inclusive hotel with her Mexican boyfriend. Lucía was determined to spend what was left over after plane tickets and everything else to see her country before she left it. I, too, saw more of Cuba that spring. My visa would expire at the end of June.

If Luis Buñuel were to take a pencil and a pad of paper and sketch out a lush countryside, it might look very similar to Cuba's. There are highways that halt mid-road with no signage to announce the asphalt's end, horses and buggies that clop along the shoulders, and rioting plants that climb power lines. Fields are tilled by oxen and skinny yipping farmers as double-decker tour buses filled with sunburned Europeans roar past. When I boarded a bus to Ciego, away from what could be called Havana's suburbs, I saw a white bridge that stretched over the highway with no onramps on either side and a man standing in the shade of a large tree with a white bandage around his head, waving his arms back and forth slowly, urgency leached from his motions. A billboard in the middle of a field with no power lines exhorted citizens to save energy. The two young adults in the seat in front of me went over what they would say at a Christian mass that Sunday. A woman six seats up cackled every few minutes throughout the six-hour ride.

Ciego was a low, spread-out town. The houses along the main road were set back from the sidewalk like animals on haunches, their front paw columns extended over the sidewalk to offer shade. The styles varied: Some were sixties mod with geometric shapes, painted mint green; others were ornate, faux-colonial confections in shades of pink and yellow. The colors were uniformly washed out. The propaganda became less pointedly directed at the *yanquis* than in Havana. There were no images of George W. Bush, but "Our Heroes Will Return" on a star with five points bore the faces of the five imprisoned spies, and "Fair Ideas Are Invincible" was scrawled alongside an image of Fidel drawing up plans for the Moncada attack.

Lucía and I walked through town, chasing the shade with our weekend bags slung over our shoulders. We took detours so she could show me the park where she'd hung out with her middle-school friends and the local branch of the Coppelia ice cream parlor, and we arrived at her parents' house in the late afternoon. A wooden door with ridges that had turned to cracks down the middle opened onto a dark front parlor and then the room where her parents slept. From there, the house circled an interior patio. Lucía's father was working in his shop out back and her mother had just begun to make dinner. After introductions, Lucía took over stirring the spaghetti while her mother, a short woman with stern hazel eyes, made sandwiches for us to take to the beach the next day. Then she took a plastic bag of rice and, after carefully folding back the frayed tablecloth from half of the dining room table, poured its contents onto the wood. I observed for a moment and then joined her work. We sat side by side and used the pads of our fingers to separate white rice grains from the small chunks of gravel and bits of chaff, pushing each into two piles.

The next morning, Lucía and I hitched four rides to reach Cayo Guillermo: a hotel employee shuttle, a pink-and-white vintage Ford, and a delivery van with rusty refrigerators clanking in the back, and then, finally, we slid into the front seat of a tourist minivan full of confused Brits, on their way from their all-inclusive resort to the secluded beach.

And after we'd shown our paid day passes and given our *carnet* numbers to the police, the beach was a postcard. Fine white sand and translucent water, perfect neon blue to the horizon. Lucía was the only local and was rewarded with free gifts from the other Cubans who staffed the facilities: the initial rides, but also complimentary beach loungers and extra beers. We left late in the afternoon in the back seat of a car driven by a tanned, elderly Italian man who'd already spent three weeks at a hotel on the cay. He dropped us at the gas station where we'd meet the employee van at six.

The next day, we cooked with Lucía's mother and visited her cousins, ate ice cream with her brother at Coppelia, watched a movie on TV, and toured Ciego on bicycles. People moved around Ciego on bikes, which was considered the lowest, most disdained form of transportation in Havana. Since there had been little gas during the Special Period, bikes were the main form of transportation through the nineties and were now a painful reminder of deprivation and degradation. If you didn't have the money even for bus fare, you rode a bicycle. In Ciego, one young couple in faded T-shirts sat up straight on separate steeds, arms draped around one another's shoulders as they pedaled along. I saw only one CUC store, which sold rum and soap and TuKola. There was no dollar option at Coppelia the way there was in Havana. Everyone waited in the same line.

Her brother, Jorge, told me a story as we waited for a table. He leaned against the iron railing as he spoke, his hand wrapped around the spike at its top. Once, when he took a group of Canadian tourists on an excursion into Ciego from Cayo Coco, he noticed a mother and her daughter quietly sobbing in the back of the bus as they rode back to the hotel. He approached them, weaving his way down the aisle, and asked them what was wrong.

She shook her head, as if she didn't want to tell him what was wrong, but continued to whimper while consoling her young daughter. He shrugged and went back to the front of the bus.

Ten minutes later, he looked back again and saw that they were still crying. Again he spoke to them, asking if anything had happened—if they were hurt, or felt sick, or if anything had been stolen. The mother shook her head tragically. I imagined the furrow of her brow, the mournful cast of her eyes.

"It's just . . . the poverty . . . it's so sad. I don't know how to explain it to my daughter," she sighed as Jorge watched from his crouched position in the aisle. Here he almost knelt toward the pavement of the sidewalk. The people in front of us in line shuffled a few inches away. "Never, not even in Haiti, have I seen such abject poverty."

At this, Jorge said, he stood up and began to talk. His knees locked as he stood now and raised his hands like a conductor. He didn't mean to, he said, but he was later reprimanded for giving a political discourse on the tour bus back to the hotel. There was apparent poverty and then there was what you couldn't see, he said. Cubans were educated and waltzed into any hospital they wanted at any time and went to museums practically for free. There were plumbing systems and rural schools and free art universities and, yes, the ration book was inadequate, but at least everyone got seven pounds of rice per month. There was no comparison with Haiti.

"I mean, Haiti? This is worse than Haiti?" he said, gesturing at the spherical topiaries at the door and the melting piles of ice cream in bowls. We were now at the entrance. "It turned out the lady had never even been to Haiti! She was talking about what she'd seen on TV." We walked toward a table.

I woke up the following morning as Lucía's mother arrived home with shopping bags: two faded plastic soda bottles that she'd refilled with juice and a Tupperware of bread.

"Looks like breakfast," I said.

"Communist sweetbread."

She giggled.

"Yes, Communist. We call things that are bad or cheaply made 'Communist.' This juice is Communist, too. See?"

She poured me a glass and I pulled off a piece of the thin, sweet, gooey bread.

"*Dale, vamos,*" Lucía said to me as she walked into the kitchen and over to her mother.

"If it's good, could we call it 'capitalist'?" I asked as I finished chewing. "This bread's pretty good. It's Sweden or something. Some socialist but also capitalist."

Her face broke into a smile as she shook her head. Lucía laughed, then put her arm around her mother and nuzzled her neck. For a few moments, there was no sound but me and her mother, reaching our fingers stickily into the Tupperware and emerging with chunks of bread between them.

"Idiots." Lucía broke the silence as she raised her head. "Everyone wants to live in Sweden. But right now we have to go *formar cola* at the train station"—wait in line to pick up the numbers that would give us seats for the crowded bus ride back west. We hopped on our bikes, went to the station, returned home for lunch, and then left.

As we sat on the bus, huddling together in the aggressive air conditioning and piling on all of the clothes we had with us as the sun dipped down, Lucía told me that her mother enjoyed visiting her in Havana, but enjoyed returning to Ciego, too. There was less to worry about in the country for an upper-middle-class Cuban: there were food co-ops of sorts, relationships with farmers just outside town who traded pigs for shoes. There weren't as many occasions to spend the CUC that her father and brother made in tips out on Cayo Coco. Worries that Lucía was beginning to consider as she planned her departure—paying rent and health care and dealing, if she had kids, with sending them to schools—weren't on Jorge's radar. There weren't as many police around; the CDR meetings that her mother had attended, she said, revolved more around neighborhood beautification than snitching. Less *resolviendo* was required. Many of Lucía's childhood friends had stayed close to home. Of course if you were poor you were still screwed, and maybe even more so than in Havana—hurricanes tore through and ruined houses and you couldn't put them back up, and then what could you do—but for families like hers, things weren't so bad. There was less of the daily indignity of being the second-most-important nationality in Cuba.

That night, the baseball playoffs were ending. Havana's Industriales team was playing Villa Clara at an away game and television sets city-wide were tuned to the same station. Every time the Industriales scored, cheers floated through the streets. Every time a fight broke out in the stands, shouts and laughter bubbled through open windows. Every time they were scored on, yelps and boos could be heard everywhere. After a few days in the countryside, the game seemed more of a metaphor than anything else: a long, drawn-out struggle between the country and its capital.

/// I took a different route every time I walked to the Plaza Vieja in Old Havana from the capitol building, where the *máquinas* dropped passengers. The plaza was in the restored section of Habana Vieja where the buildings looked like pastries with white curlicued rosettes, a Disneyland of Spanish colonial architecture restored by the Office of the Historian of

the City of Havana. The historian, Eusebio Leal, had worked out a deal: A portion of the profits made in the tourist corridor funded further neighborhood restorations. From a fiscal perspective, Old Havana was a tiny functioning town within the greater city proper. Wooden scaffolding increasingly appeared on blocks ever farther from its core. Leal's economic scheme was widely seen as an eventual model for the rest of the city: a socialist mid-point that incentivized profit while maintaining government oversight.

The border between the renovated area and what hadn't yet been fixed was unmarked but unmistakable. The streets of the unrestored old town looked, at first glance, to be a mess of pocked facades and *barbacoas*—makeshift lofts that residents had installed in rooms with colonial double-height ceilings. Entire swaths of the area just behind the Plaza Vieja, which had *kook*-charging restaurants and a new Cuervo y Sobrinos luxury watch shop, had no running water. Children in droopy school uniforms carried buckets in the streets. A chaos of power lines burst from each building, reaching to invite electricity into rooms that hadn't been rewired for over half a century. Doorbells had long since given up, so people stood in streets and cupped hands around mouths. The only public parks were the size of buildings that had surrendered, crumpled to the floor and left holes occupied now by kids with big ears and knobby elbows and patched-up baseballs. The area was disorienting: The unbroken shades of dusty gray buildings all looked the same and the ocean wasn't visible.

To make Old Havana's atmospheric, sagging buildings safe for Cuban residents was an unarguably positive undertaking. Yet as renovators swept through and some people were removed from their crumbling homes, sent to Soviet-style apartment blocks beyond La Lisa or back to the rural provinces they'd illegally come from, something was lost both intellectually and aesthetically. Every building that sported new tiles, historically accurate colonnades, and trompe l'oeil moldings replaced a pocket of the city's reality with ersatz Havana, a monument to nostalgia and denial, a dictated version of historical accuracy made brighter by more potent paints. I could think of nothing more American in essence, nothing more realistic and prosaic and capitalist than Old Havana as it swapped in a chocolate store where an apartment block had been, as it swathed buildings in cheery pinks and yellows.

Backstreets, by contrast, felt anarchic and promising. Over time, their elegance emerged. I found a late-sixties bar, with blue velvet stools and windows shaped like ship's portholes that were filled with fish, which was never open when I wanted a daiquiri. I saw a hulking art nouveau apartment building with boarded-up windows and balconies shaped like climbing vines and I discovered an unmarked antique shop packed with the treasures of dying old dames, where I found a tiny tin notebook with an orange enamel cover. The first page read *Movies Seen by Me in the Year 1933.* Old Havana was decrepit and unfair and ersatz, but also exciting, rewarding, romantic, tempting.

The idea of staying in Havana was tempting. I could return to my Communist fairy godfather and ask to extend my visa. It'd be cheaper to stay in Havana to write than to move back to Mexico City or to New York or some unknown destination. Elaine nursed these fantasies on Saturday afternoons as we cooked golden *malanga* fritters while Carlos pulled out old family photos. "How can you leave? You'll miss it too much," she said. "It'll break your heart. Ours, too. And we'll be going in just another year. You should go back with us then."

But staying in Havana meant accepting being asked to leave at any moment. Most long-term foreigners had considered what they would do if someone rapped at their door at eight in the morning and told them they'd be on the evening flight back to wherever they'd come from. Every expat in Havana knows at least one person to whom this has happened, including the European businessman in his early forties who lived with his family in a tasteful Playa home, who hosted a dinner party I attended with Katherine a month before my visa was due to expire. We ate amid the palms and low candles, chattering of art and politics, when the question arose of what he would do if a MinInt agent arrived at his house. It would be impossible to dismantle their home quickly, the man said, matter-of-factly. He'd leave it all behind if it came to that.

He clarified: He would take his family and as much of the artwork he'd bought in Cuba as possible, he said. They had already stored family heirlooms and photo albums at the small apartment they kept in their hometown. He knew which friend could help him pack without being incriminated by association, who had another SUV he could borrow to drive as many big suitcases to the airport as possible, and how much money to leave the maid so she'd have enough to live on until she found work again.

When an expat moves away from Cuba under normal circumstances—a new diplomatic assignment, a move back to company headquarters—state agents inspect everything that will be shipped out of the country. They ensure that there's no Cuban patrimony, antiques, old paintings, or anything of historical value, and that the list of objects being taken out matches the list of objects brought into the country. In decades past, *gusanos* who left Cuba hid wedding rings under shoe insoles, swallowed their savings in gold nuggets, were allowed to board flights with only the clothes they wore. Today, they can bring suitcases but no objects. Elaine was selling everything she'd acquired over the years slowly so as not to attract attention, and I wanted to buy her coffee table for my U.S. apartment, to start my life there with something of hers.

"Is it a sculpture by a modern artist? Because only contemporary art can be taken from the country," said a lipsticked bureaucrat at *patrimonio*, which granted permits for art export.

"Even if a Cuban is legally leaving the country? Like a musician or an artist, going to Europe for a fellowship?" I asked. I ran through the cast of people I knew of whom I could ask favors, who'd help *resolver*.

The woman, who'd worn a leopard-print blouse and waved herself with a fan, shook her head mournfully. "No one, *mi cielo*, no, no, no. You see, there's a scarcity of furniture here in Cuba. Nothing can leave." Only what had been brought in by foreigners could be taken back out.

"*Mm-hmm*," said Carlos with pursed lips and raised eyebrows when I came home sighing. "Everything is theirs. Not even our furniture is ours. *Que fuerte.*"

Elaine had labeled everything in their apartment: the blender, refrigerator, toaster, rice cooker, cabinet, and most pantry items were emblazoned with small pieces of pink paper with black English lettering. If I was really leaving, she wanted to be able to ask me pronunciation tips for my last month.

"Sugar," I'd say.

"Sucer," Elaine would repeat.

"Shoo-ger," I'd shake my head.

She waved a hand over her shoulder as she walked to the other end of the kitchen. Lucía had come over and she, Elaine, Carlos, Nicolas, and I shared a bottle of wine and some Cuban Camembert I'd found at Le Select. Lucía hadn't yet booked a flight for Chile. Her visa would expire in three months.

"The one thing I know I'll really have a hard time

adjusting to," she said as she walked back, "is the way that people socialize up there. You all work all the time and only spend time together when you make plans in advance."

"Also, something's going to happen here as soon as you leave," Elaine said, waving one of her three daily cigarettes around the table.

We stared.

"Here in Havana, here, both of you. Because you're both leaving, aren't you?" she said, impatient. "I've never seen it like this before. There's a strange energy right now. There's no rice in Havana."

There was no 3 *kook* rice in *la chopin*, thinning piles of bodega rice at inflated prices at the *agro*, people hoarding what they could because the government hadn't paid the company they imported the rice from, or something. State preschools were being given flour for kids' lunches.

There was more, too, she said slowly. Rumors of new laws were floating around—that university graduates would not be granted exit visas under any circumstances, for one, that cell phone charges would increase to stem the tide of Cubans who owned them. The requisites for entering university were becoming more difficult, with a mandatory mathematics test that was tough to pass with the preparation students received at state schools. In order to send kids to college, *guajiros* might have to hire tutors.

Nicolas nodded. The heat of the summer was when things always got desperate, he said. Summer heat lifted the difference between Elaine's cross-ventilation and Sandra's baking shed to transparent and unbridgeable. Heat settled like an iron cloud. Even the *playas del este* were collective bathtubs, too warm, too many limbs.

There had been a mass exodus of people from Cuba, he continued, during summers while both of the Democratic

U.S. presidents before Obama had been in office. The Mariel boat-lift in 1980 took place under Jimmy Carter, and the *balsero* crisis of 1994 had led Bill Clinton to institute the "wet foot, dry foot" policy.

"We're overdue at this point," said Elaine.

But, I said, that very week I had walked by an Old Havana building under construction, asked what it was, and was told by a guard that it would be a school for new Ministry of the Interior recruits. And Raúl had increased the numbers of police in the streets. We hadn't noticed because the increase had been gradual, but young policemen with the puffed-out chests of new recruits were on nearly every street corner now. Inertia, I said slowly. I thought inertia would reign.

Havana was a mirror. Elaine needed to believe that other Cubans were as dissatisfied as she. Liberal Americans, who pointed rigid fingers at health care and rations as evidentiary claims, wanted to believe that market-driven capitalist ideology wasn't the only possible political system after the fall of the U.S.S.R. Conservatives cited government repression, inadequate rations, and crippling bureaucracy as proof that, really, it was. The over-scheduled and over-networked tourists who came from the world's capital cities to visit saw improbably happy Cubans. "It's astonishing; they're poor but happy," I'd overheard a tourist saying at a Chinatown restaurant that week. "We could all learn from them to value what's really important." If I saw inertia, it was because somewhere I hoped for it. Everyone was, of course, partially right.

/// Adrián would leave a month after I did, for a town in Holland that had given him a government grant to study music. We sat in the Miami Vice gleam of the bar at Miramar's Hotel Panorama, built in 2002 but sweating eighties cool. Adrián played piano in the lobby a few afternoons a week. We ordered mojitos from a waitress in a tight navy suit. He told me how in Europe, he wouldn't have to study classical composition at all to get his master's. He had never actually gotten his ISA degree, but he'd get a master's. See—it was pure jazz, pure avant-garde, pure improv.

Adrián's position on his success had changed in the last year. "What have the last two years of my life been?" he repeated my question back to me. "Lots of luck without so much work. A complete loss of innocence. Before, the idea of being good and successful was more idealistic for me. But no matter how I feel, I need jobs."

This was part of why he was going to Europe. As a handsome light-skinned black man, he could lean on exoticism as well as talent to push him along. He toyed with the mint in his mojito as he spoke of what he'd learned recently, and what he hoped to learn abroad: "How people act, how they work, how I can use different masks and faces—different personas."

In Cuba, he had always known how to alternate hypocrisy and earnestness, how to flip from one into the other. What he hadn't known was how to tailor his persona to the people who surrounded him, how to talk to businesspeople and then musicians, how to be a chameleon. This was what he hoped to master now, he said. But I thought he was also leaving because he'd finally come to see in his success too much of the arbitrary, too much privilege granted by the Cuban condition, and he wanted to test himself elsewhere. If he stayed, it might break his heart. He'd be back—he'd always be back, and he wasn't breaking up with his girlfriend, so he'd be back soon, even—but for now, he needed to leave.

The grant Adrián had gotten was exactly the sort that Adela wanted to find but couldn't: She had no Internet connection now and wouldn't spend her mother's CUC on hotel Internet hours. Adela was living in Havana again and had a handsome lawyer boyfriend, but he would go meet his family in Elizabeth, New Jersey, within the next two months. She'd tried to keep herself distant but she'd fallen in love with him, and now every conversation they had ended in tears. The loneliness she knew she'd feel when he left loomed. She'd have married him if he asked but it wouldn't happen, she said, it'd wrench up all of the plans that were already in place.

Adela's brother had left two months ago, disappeared one day and then, after they hadn't heard from him for a week, sent an email. He was in Ecuador. After two years of trying legal means, he'd hopped a skiff to the Yucatan, made his way through Mexico and down to Ecuador. They'd spoken on the phone once or twice, but he wouldn't tell her anything. He didn't want to remember what had happened to him on the journey, he said.

Nothing had changed, except that now there seemed to be idiocy rather than nobility behind striving for and, worse, claiming to have achieved perfect consensus among citizens. The closer any of her nascent questioning got to the core of that consensus, Adela saw, the more everything she'd thought she'd known looked different. And even so, Old Havana retained its cheery pastel storefronts, Miramar its graceful avenues, El Caribeño its university mojitos, the book fair its inexpensive paperbacks. Her friends still threw the occasional house party and children still played gleefully in the parks, dusty and bruised from running too fast. Adela had grown up running in the streets, her parents unworried back at home. She could have asked anyone in her building—no, on her block, in her neighborhood, in all of Havana, it felt like—for a glass of water on a hot day without the tension and strain of worries. She'd heard that houses in regular suburbs in Mexico had walls two stories high, and kidnappings. She knew about the pedophiles and teenagers who brought guns into middle schools in the United States. Adela's eyes said she'd expected more from the world, and more from adulthood. Her mouth kept moving, talking, smiling taut twitchy smiles.

She would wait until the end of the year, once her social service was done, to ask for her *papeles de liberación*. "How ridiculous," she said, "that we have to wait to be 'liberated.' I never imagined that I'd want to live any part of my life anywhere else. But almost everyone I know has left or is leaving. You want to know what I think about the youth today? The youth of today are *gone*."

/// Sometimes it's by consensus that we move on: At some point, like Lucía, you're the oldest person in the room and the party no longer seems quite so fun. Reckless hope feels more reckless than hopeful; the anxiety of an inevitable but unclear future feels less glittery than stressful; being held at a starting gate generates no potential speed and only frustration. The twinned yearnings of both young adulthood and post-Fidel Havana could, as I had discovered, generate a perfect fervor. But Lucía felt old around people for whom Havana was still golden in its imperfection and possibility.

Havana was the frenzy of heat and the relief of a dive into water, or hitchhiking from the *playas del este* to downtown, waiting in sandy feet and a damp bikini on the side of the road, knowing it'd take two hours to travel the twenty miles but not much caring. Living in Havana had, for me, been a sense of simultaneous discovery and impotence, a monolith of governmental control Swiss-cheesed with resourcefulness, grace and squalor, yearning and resignation, passion, anesthesia, innocence, and cynicism. And leaving Havana was walking out of a movie before its final scene. But the movie was too long and the climax never seemed to arrive. The old wooden armrests bit into elbows and the *cucuruchos* of pea-nuts and popcorn had long since been eaten. The experience was engrossing, magnetic, until suddenly the nagging sense of the day diminishing on the other side of the doors became impossible to ignore.

I flew out when my visa expired; the last time Lucía saw Claudio was at her good-bye parties, just before she left at the end of the summer.

10

NEXT YEAR IN HAVANA

On my first visit to Cuba—it was 2003, and I was twenty—I'd left my passport on the small plane that ferried me from Miami to Havana. I had stared out at the countryside, at palm trees stiff and shaggy-headed over the tangle of fields around the airport, at the red earth paths that sliced between one emerald swath and another of paler green. I was so entranced that my passport remained tucked into the pocket of the seat-back in front of me after I'd gotten off the plane. In the line at immigration, I realized my mistake. Dropping my bags on the faux marble floor next to the people I'd traveled with, family friends, I slipped past the men and women in green military uniforms with plastic epaulettes at their shoulders. No one stopped me as I began to run. I sprinted toward the plane, sandals flapping down the tarmac, diesel fuel in my nostrils. A flight attendant met me at the bottom of the stairs, shaking his head. He held up my little blue book. "Lucky girl," he'd said as I bent over to catch my breath, one hand on my knee and the other gripping my passport.

In 2011 I was among the first to get off the plane and knew by then where I was going, so I was the first to hit the brown-and-tan plastic immigration cabins. Inside each was a man or woman in a green uniform with plastic epaulettes, sitting under the hanging cameras for which the guards would ask me not to smile. I handed over my tourist visa, the first I'd had in more than two years, and looked into the security camera.

At the X-ray station, where agents ensure that no one brings illegal taxable products into the country, someone tapped my shoulder. "Julia? Give me your passport."

A man in a short-sleeved button-down shirt told me to wait. Passengers began to trickle out. A Mexican woman from my flight lost her scarf. She glared at the uniformed man behind the X-ray machine, who held up his hands defensively. What would he want with a scarf? A tourist called out: It was stuck under the moving track.

Another man in a khaki uniform touched my shoulder. He held my passport in his hands.

He waved me to follow him as he wound through the baggage claim crowd, a strange, silent ballet. When we stopped, I asked him in Spanish what was going on. He told me to get my bags and come find him. He'd keep my passport.

"A random search," he called out over his shoulder in English.

I had recently moved to New York and Lucía was in Chile. "Half the world has congratulated me for leaving Cuba," Lucía told me a few weeks after arriving in Santiago. "It's as if I'd gotten out of jail." It was as if she'd joined a club that hung in a loose crochet around the world, Cubans everywhere who'd made the same choice as she. Within her first two weeks, she got a job and saw a 3-D movie for the first time. She had to leave to throw up after half an hour of Shrek II. "I'm just a simple *guajira*," she told me over Skype, laughing.

There'd been personal change, yes, but that year also brought a slow introduction of grinding change to Cuba: During the summer of 2010, fifty-two dissidents had been released from jail. In September, the Cuban congress passed a raft of three hundred economic reforms that would, over the course of the next five years, move one-fifth of the state's five million workers into private business, free up state businesses from party and government administration, authorize Cubans to buy and sell homes and cars, decentralize some decision-making, and decrease dependence on the state via rations and state meals. The implementation of these changes had already begun and, officials promised, would continue to layer one shift atop another. Among the first was the legalization of 178 non-professional jobs, among them "handyman," "hair stylist," "button-upholsterer," and "clown." For the first time, any activity that the government hadn't trained someone to do at a university, which didn't involve buying and reselling the same goods in Cuba, could be practiced legally. And simultaneous leadership shake-ups at some of the country's biggest companies had put military men in positions of power. Over ten members of Raúl's cabinet, too, were now Cuban military. That March 2011, the last two political prisoners who'd been arrested in 2003's "Black Spring" were released. The American USAID contractor was still in jail, and in October, international businessmen would begin to be jailed, too, on charges of corruption and possible espionage. It was a simultaneous contraction into ever more isolation at the top and a loosening at the bottom.

My three bags surrounded me as I considered the questions that the guard posed casually, though he stood straight and tall: I'd been to Cuba before, hadn't I? When? What years, months had I spent here? What did I study? Where had

I lived? Where was I staying this time? The man was about my age, with shoulders that fit perfectly into his plain khaki uniform, neither scrawny nor gym-built. He had light skin and dark hair and looked like someone I might have flirted with at the University of Havana when I'd studied there. I was on vacation, I told him. Okay, and where was I staying? With Carlos, I thought, and tried to remember the address of a casa particular. Foreigners still had to be registered somewhere, and this knowledge bleached all logic from my mind. The casa on San Lazaro where I used to live, I could have said, or even the Hotel Riviera, with its diamond-shaped pool. But despite these proper responses, with addresses and names out of my mind's reach, I told him I would stay with a friend. His questions sharpened.

Why had I come to Cuba? Who was picking me up at the airport? How did I meet this friend? Could I please spell out her full name? Did I know her phone number?

I began to measure the possible area between what he knew and what I knew: I knew academics and writers who, after publishing work critical of the regime, had been told on landing at Jose Martí International Airport that they'd be on the return flight out. I knew that I carried magazines in my bag with contents pages that listed my name on them. We both knew that I had no journalist visa.

I wrote down Katherine's name. How much money was I bringing? Credit cards? What was in my luggage?

Forty-five minutes had ticked by and no one remained in the hall but a small cluster of six men, all wearing jeans and short-sleeved button-down shirts, scowls, with no luggage and cell phones clipped to their belts. The man questioning me told me to wait a moment and he retreated to their group. He gesticulated as he read off the sheet of paper on which he'd been taking notes. No one looked my way.

He returned after a few minutes. "Follow me," he said. "Can I look in your suitcase, please? Is it heavy? Do you need help lifting it?" He bent down, lifted my duffel bag with soft chivalry, and gestured that I should roll my carryon and follow him.

The money exchange attendant flirted with a man who leaned against her counter. Their giggles echoed.

I trotted behind the guard to catch up, spilling questions as I approached him. "Will my friend get in any trouble? Is this because I am an *estadounidense*?"

"No," he said as he lifted the first of my two suitcases onto the inspection table. "We just want to have someplace to locate you, you know, in case of emergency, since you don't have a hotel or casa particular listed. What if there's a hurricane or something?"

He pawed through bikinis, a towel, a bag of sunscreen. He saw the shiny hair of a stuffed animal, a bottle of gummy vitamins for Juan and Alejandra's toddler, and the gigantic bag of tampons that I'd leave with women here. I simpered: Vitamins! A stuffed animal! For my Cuban friends!

He glanced at my shoes in the next bag, less interested now. Then he saw the stack of four *New Yorkers* and a Czech novel that I'd ordered for an expat friend online, under which lay the rest of the magazines.

"What is this book? What does the title mean? What are these? Show them to me." He flipped through magazine pages, his face stern, and then he pointed at the movie listings. "How do you pronounce this movie, in English? It was playing at Cine Acapulco last week."

He helped me zip my bags back up and sent me out the sliding doors and into Cuba.

"I was afraid you'd slipped past me," Katherine said, releasing the arms she'd been clutching. We got into her car, and I told her why I was late. "Yes," she said as she flicked on the radio and rolled down the window, "that happens. It's happened to all of us."

We headed back to her place, where we drank fresh mango juice. The bird-of-paradise bushes in the garden were flowering, red and fuchsia, and all the doors of the house were open and everywhere it smelled like fresh-cut grass and oranges. I would stay with her for a few days while I figured out what to do. Hours later, I had read half a novel in the garden with my feet up, taken a cool shower in the hot afternoon with the wind blowing through the bathroom. Everything before that moment had washed off me. Why wouldn't someone have interrogated me at the airport? Why wouldn't I have been shown that I was being kept tabs on, and then allowed to enter the country? I was back in Havana.

/// The most visible consequences of the economic reforms were hand-painted signs for new businesses all over the city: a seamstress, someone who sold handmade candles for Santería ceremonies, hundreds of small cafés that peddled mediocre food, a few good in-home restaurants. Women in doorways sold more than just 1-peso *cafecitos* now: You could buy cookies and sweets, a sandwich from a snack stand. For the first time since I'd begun going to Havana eight years earlier, I spent no time hungry out of the sheer impossibility of finding food to purchase at certain hours of the day. There were even late-night cafeterias.

A year of renovations had left Katherine's walls shimmery silver, her paintings hung, her roof replaced. Isnael had gotten a new tattoo of a scorpion on his left shoulder, just above the meat of his shoulder muscles, because he was a Scorpio. He was still saving to make saint, he said, though he didn't look like someone who was trying to save money:

He wore new shoes and had acquired a cell phone. He knew which neighborhood cafés sold the best cheap food to bring home for dinner. These days, he spent more time as a companion to Katherine's son than as anything else. Renovation materials were still tightly controlled, so there wasn't much for him to do around the house. We sat on her couch one afternoon and he tinkered with her PlayStation console. He'd become pretty good at a certain warcraft game, he said, and it was hard for me to tear his attention from the screen once he began to play, to show me his newly acquired skills. He didn't understand the English directions on the screen, though, and kept killing his allies.

I visited with the punk rockers and learned that Liván didn't hang out with Takeshi anymore, because Takeshi had gotten more emo than punk, which offended him. I brought my computer to his house one afternoon to show him the image my photographer friend had taken of them on our night out so long ago; Liván had been almost nineteen then, and his features had begun to soften as he'd grown up and gained weight. His mother, Bertha, leaned over my shoulder. "See how good he looks," she crooned. She patted his head and he pulled away. The only thing that had changed other than Liván's sharp jaw and his group of friends was the quantity of tattoos he had. He'd gotten a few new ones, including a large, sickly green image of SpongeBob SquarePants that slid down his calf. He liked *Bob Esponja* because "I don't know, he's the most *loco* of the cartoons," he said with a shrug. It was professional-looking and new, with precise lines and subtle colors, not just black and red in blurry lines like the PUNK FULA on his wrist or the ANARQUIA on his knuckles. Tattoo artist: newly legal.

"They just want to go to G Street, all of them," said Adela of her students. She was still teaching philosophy at the university. She said that today's nineteen-year-old college kids simply tuned out for anything that had to do with Marx, which was half of the state-mandated syllabus. There was no engaging them. They sat on G Street and drank or they flirted and went home with each other, and that was it. We sat in her bedroom and she pointed at a book by Marx on her shelf and said, "He was a sociologist and an important figure. They should know who he is, at least. But G Street is all they do."

Adela hadn't left Cuba. I had often wondered, in the year since I'd left Havana, if I really knew who Adela was. Journalists had been duped by pro-Castro revolutionaries in the past, the most famous being Manuel David Orrio, a spy who'd posed as an dissident journalist long enough to be profiled in the *Chicago Tribune* and denounce a handful of real dissidents who wound up in jail. The paper retracted the profile when he tore off his mask to jeer at those who had believed his pose, crying tears of joy on state television at the anti-Castro activists who'd been put in jail by his testimony. They were his recompense for years of lies. Once, drunk at a party with Lucía, a friend of hers had slurred to me that no one around me was who they said they were. He'd dated an American and the secret police had knocked on his door the day after she'd spent the night for the first time to interrogate him. I'd dismissed his words as boozy hyperbole, but the reality was, any one of my sources could have been someone spinning false stories of spliced families and sodden dreams.

We drank our sweet espresso and headed into the kitchen to make more. She'd heard that changes were happening in Havana, she said, with sarcasm that promised me she knew the new rules to the letter. But the change that she pointed out to me as she spooned coffee into the espresso maker was that the government agriculture ministry was blending its *bodega* coffee with ground peas. Coffee production was down this year. "You know what we call it?" she said with a dry laugh. "Osama bin Laden: It can explode the coffee maker and cut you up."

The tourism ministry, at least, reported swelling numbers: A 13 percent increase in revenue from tourists in 2011, with a year-long revenue of $2.5 billion, had boosted the formal economy. But that June, Sandra wasn't seeing any of it. We had met at nearly exactly the same spot of our first meeting. It had been tough to find clients lately, she said, and her new Cuban boyfriend, sitting next to her on the *malecón*, nodded. "I've been here last night, the night before, all last weekend, and nothing," she said. She dabbed her forehead with an orange washcloth so she looked dewy but never damp. The boy shook his head. He was a cute *mulatico*, short and skinny with an Ed Hardy baseball hat. Sandra gestured toward the Riviera and the Meliá Cohiba on the opposite corner: "See how few lights are on?" She was brusque and stiff, as if her insides had puddled down and a shell kept her upright. "Not even worth paying to get in."

Though it was legal to open small businesses like salons, Sandra couldn't fall back on her beautician training because a neighbor with a quicker reaction time already had a monopoly on her block. Gallego was in jail, seven years on charges Sandra wouldn't detail. Mia was nearly two and back home with Aboo, same as always, doing fine. No sign of the Italian. But I could come over tomorrow. She'd call when she woke up. "That'd be great," I said. Before I left, she asked me for money. Just $5 or maybe $10 or whatever, just so she could get a cab home.

Whatever change was happening in Cuba, taking place at the top and promising a downward trickle, it hadn't reached these people yet. Their lives still seemed like snow globes shaken by someone else.

I didn't have much cash on me but I handed Sandra a $5 bill and walked away, feeling like there was a fire at my back and I was gliding toward the air that fed it. She never called the number I gave her.

/// My small apartment had been rented to a Chilean, so I shared Carlos's room with him. *"Estás flaca y amarilla,"* were his first words to me when I arrived. Thin and yellow.

His second words were, "What do you want to drink?" He stalked toward the kitchen. "I have water, juice, cola, coffee?" He posed half in the living room, one eyebrow raised and his hand resting expectantly on his hip.

Elaine and Nicolas had gone to Miami two months earlier and left the boys in Havana. Maykel had gotten out of his military service, but six months later he'd been in a minor car accident in his rented gypsy cab. One sudden Saturday morning just after Elaine and Nicolas had interviewed at the U.S. Interests Section and been given their visas, an acquaintance had rapped at the door of their Miramar apartment. The owner of the car was going to press charges, though Nicolas had already repaired the car himself. The family friend felt wronged, I supposed, and knew that Elaine and Nicolas had been saving. If they waited until the following week, they'd probably not get to Miami for months, if ever—until the legal proceedings had wrapped up. Nicolas went to the airport to see if the two of them could fly to Miami that night, before government offices opened on Monday. He could better help his son by sending out money from the U.S. to pay off the car's owner than by sticking around to show up in court. In the end, Elaine had eight hours to pack and leave.

We'd spoken on the phone frequently since she arrived.

"*Ey, niña,* you have to check on the boys and report back," Elaine ordered me. "From the emails everyone sends me, it sounds like they're doing well. It seems what they needed all along was to live without me."

Carlos had his own Interests Section appointment for November 2012, but he hoped he wouldn't make it. The first day I saw him, he'd just returned from the Brazilian embassy. He vibrated with excitement. He was applying for a scholarship to study in one of the country's smaller cities, a grant that, the woman at the embassy said, the Cuban government had prohibited them from advertising widely in Cuba. He'd heard about it through a friend of a friend. "All the better for my chances," he said with a grin as he paced the apartment. I sat in a chair under one of the plants, in front of the floor-to-ceiling frosted-glass jalousie blinds. The living room felt cavernous: The dining room table and chairs, two sofas, a coffee table, and the wicker set that Nicolas sanded each year and Elaine had painstakingly painted a fresh white all had been sold. We drank water out of cheap glasses, not Elaine's fifties metallic polka-dotted ones—she'd managed to get rid of nearly everything.

In Brazil, Carlos would be given free tuition at a school where he could study, among other subjects, film, advertising, or design. Elaine's sister lived in a small town in the North and as long as Carlos didn't defect, their apartment would stay in the family. He could rent it for money to support himself. His plans glimmered, hazy skyscraper fantasies cloaked in mist. The paperwork was under way.

Elaine was not happy. A care package she'd sent recently contained socks for Carlos, toothbrushes (the only ones for sale in Cuba were rough on the gums), and DVDs with photos. Here were Elaine, Nicolas, and Carlos's cousins at the mall; at a pool party; next to an open grill with all kinds of beef on it; in front of an open trunk, the handles of white plastic grocery bags fluttering.

She wanted him to keep his Interests Section appointment and join them in Miami. As his plans solidified, as paperwork was processed and airfares were researched, she became increasingly convinced that hers would be yet another Cuban family split across the borders of so many countries. But Carlos didn't want to move to the United States with so little English, with no degree, with no experience doing anything but getting by and having fun in Havana.

One afternoon, Carlos called my cell phone as I walked away from the underground antique store to which I thought Elaine had sold much of her vintage glassware.

"I need to tell you something important but it's too expensive to talk on the cell," he said, his voice deep with tension. "Call me from a land line, because I'm freaking out. Ay, no, never mind, just come home."

In the fifteen-minute *máquina* ride, my thoughts unraveled beneath the passenger chatter. Men in button-down shirts, MinInt, my magazines, Carlos's apartment, the same stale story.

I found Carlos chain-smoking and jittery. We sat at the kitchen table and he told me that a cousin of Elaine's and her husband had come over. She had asked for coffee and he had dropped a stuffed backpack on the floor.

"We're not leaving," the husband said to Carlos. "When you leave, this apartment should be ours, not yours and not the government's, but in order for that to happen, we have to live here first. I'll sleep here even if it's on the floor."

When Carlos said no, that the apartment was his, the cousin began to shout. "We know that you're doing things that shouldn't be done here. We know that you're renting to a foreigner in the back," she cried, "and we'll call the police."

Carlos told them to leave and never to come back, but he was shaken. If the cousin followed through, not only could Carlos lose his family's apartment, but the exit permits for his brother and himself would be in jeopardy. Why would the government do a favor, handing out passports and exit visas, for a citizen who'd flouted its laws?

Carlos's hands trembled as he lit one cigarette after another. His brother was in the back telling the Chilean that he'd have to find other accommodations.

As we talked, we understood: This was why Elaine wanted him to come to the United States instead of going to Brazil on a scholarship. If he went to Brazil, he wouldn't be starting new elsewhere, he would be on a temporary leave. And Elaine was tired of fighting, of being a Cuban in Cuba.

Carlos would, like Lucía, go to whichever country gave him a visa first. It didn't wind up taking so long, but if the process had stretched out, elongated a year and a half, Carlos wouldn't have needed to get an exit visa in the first place. The blanket requirement for exit visas for all Cuban citizens would be among the next large changes to be implemented. Exit visas had been put in place by a government, in 1961, that saw so many of its most valuable citizens leaving that it feared a mass exodus. Fifty years later, the *tarjeta blanca* was dismantled by a slightly different government, one that knew that those who'd had the enterprise to seek exit visas would still be the citizens who could afford to leave without the requirement. Prices for passports and plane tickets and entry visas to other countries hadn't changed; those who earned the average Cuban salary of $18 per month were still equally limited.

And among the 178 new careers possible for Cubans, there were no permits for engineers, architects, lawyers, doctors—professionals who'd been trained by the free revolutionary education system. Anyone deemed important to the "human capital created by the Revolution," the new law stated, could not practice independently.

The way I saw it, the closer anyone got to questioning the rhetoric that protected power, the invisible lines separating the owners from the players, the harsher the rejection. This may have applied everywhere, as much in my own country as in Cuba, but in Cuba, young people have always known it. I grew up very American, optimistic and believing that I could do something in the world if I tried hard enough. In Cuba, young people had already changed the world. The word "Revolution" had already acquired a meaning that was close enough to the present that there wasn't room for another definition.

The sense of being stuck in a maze had magnified. Among those who could benefit from the new regulations, envy was rampant: Carlos's cousin, his brother's family friend, a diplomat acquaintance who had been robbed on the streets of Miramar. Among those who wouldn't, who lacked entrepreneurial spirit or family funds from abroad or a deed to a well-placed apartment, fear was rising. So were complaints of hunger, I was told: "It's the first time since the Special Period that I've heard people saying, '*Caballero, que hambre tengo,*'" Alejandra told me one afternoon. How hungry I am. For the first time, Cubans were being told that they should be able to make it on their own. Wasn't that what people had demanded for so long? Wasn't that enough?

Maybe it would never be enough. Hope in Cuba was the desire to live in a world that didn't actually exist. In Adela's idealism, she'd thought that Cuba could be that world, as had I, at least at first. For some people, Nicolas and Lucía, abroad had always held the promise of that world, the "anyplace else" to which their hope had fled.

But hope and Cuba were a tricky combination, I thought.

There was little room in Havana for hope of the large-scale variety. That sort of hope had been all used up in the sixties. No, small-scale hope was strewn all over individuals and relationships: Isnael and the continuing negotiation between fantasy and reality in the life he was starting to make for himself; Lucía and adulthood in Chile that didn't feel quite comfortable, yet, she said, but still, it was hers to construct and it stretched out enticingly in front of her; Juan and Alejandra, the photography tours they were now planning to lead and an upcoming trip to Spain, the first time she'd travel abroad; Carlos's scholarship and Elaine and Nicolas and my ticket to visit them in Miami. I would see them in a month and we'd speculate together, hot air about what could happen next year in Havana.

EPILOGUE

AUGUST 2013

The first thing I notice—and I notice it before I even hit the ground in Cuba, in the Cubana de Aviación line at the Cancun airport—is the bling. A young couple hovers in line behind me, holding their Cuban passports and pushing two plastic-wrapped cardboard boxes, one with an image of a carseat on it and the other a stroller. The young woman wears a sizable diamond on her left ring finger. I am not quite impartial, because I am wearing a diamond ring, too: Juan, in New York for eight months on work, has asked me to bring an engagement ring to Alejandra. If it doesn't fit, there aren't jewelers that he'd trust to resize it in Havana, so he wants me to ferry it back to New York on the other end of my trip.

The ring used to belong to a Cuban woman whose husband left her when they arrived in the States shortly after the Revolution; she waited twelve years for him before going to the Washington Heights resale shop where Juan found the ring and its story. Elaine told me on the phone last night to be sure to wear it because that way I have plausible deniability and no one will make me pay taxes. Tomorrow Alejandra and I will sit on her porch and she'll slide the too-big ring along her finger and talk about the symmetry, how she has been waiting for Juan to come back from New York for so many more months than she'd anticipated. He got a single-entry visa and his project has taken longer than planned so though he's sent friends to Havana with bags of clothing, money, and this engagement ring, he can't leave the country himself. While I am in Havana, I will see diamond rings on women at the new rooftop restaurants, and strands of pearls, too, and black-and-white iPhones that sit on tables, waiting to buzz with the news of which bar everyone will be at after dinner.

The changes that have swept through are evident in different ways at Jose Martí International Airport. There is a new line at immigration, "Residentes en Cuba," and it's longer than the others. Before, there were so few Cubans traveling that they just slid into any Canadian- and Mexican-populated line. And the tourist visa no longer requests the address where the foreigner will stay. No one cares where I or anyone else will reside while in Havana anymore. At the baggage carousel, there is a trio of women in high platform heels who sweep enormous, bulky duffel bags onto carts while speaking rapid Cuban and there is a man who picks up four Hankook tires, all wrapped in plastic, while telling someone on a cell phone that he is at the baggage carousel right now and just has to pass through customs to pay taxes on the tires. He will be outside in ten minutes.

"Do not eat from any of the new street cafés, eh," Elaine admonished me. "There's cholera in Cuba but, of course, no one official is admitting it." But there are no new cafés on the streets of inland Marianao as my taxi driver takes me into the city via the back roads, and when I ask him how business has been lately, he says it's the same as it's always been except he's paying higher taxes now. There are a lot of Argentines around lately, he says, and they're annoying as hell but they're great tourists so he's not complaining.

/// Official emigration numbers held mostly steady in Cuba throughout the first decade of the twenty-first century. Things weren't as bad as the nineties and change was rippling. But emigration rose slowly and in 2012 they spiked almost as high as the statistic for 1994, the year of the rafter crisis that littered the Straits with bodies. This number—46,662—is acknowledged in accompanying news reports to be largely composed of the young and the educated. Fidel Castro's legacy, the family scattered as from a saltshaker across the globe, is the inheritance of his brother, too.

This news is announced in August, when I am in Havana. What's also announced in the foreign media is that a man sets out from the Marina Hemingway to cross the Florida Straits on a paddleboard. Twenty-eight hours later, he's made it across. I also read that seven Cubans in their forties and fifties have died in state hospitals after drinking industrial methanol, thinking it was rum. But the only news that really travels, the news that sprints laps around the city on people's lips, is that the U.S. State Department is lengthening most Cuban visitor visas from six months to five years, including multiple entries, which used to require further visa applications and $160 fees.

An era has ended in Cuba. Whether he planned to or not, Raúl has, in his half-decade tenure, implemented a Stalin-esque five-year plan. Exit visas are no longer required of Cubans who'd like to travel or leave, but also: Even before the number 46,662 is officially released, everyone is talking about the measures that the government is taking in an attempt to stanch the flow, economic reforms and then some. People can freely buy and sell cars and homes and they can keep their property if they leave. And now the length of time that someone can stay outside the country without being considered a defector has been stretched to two years, which can be provisionally lengthened another twenty-four months. You can close the door of your home for two years, now, without any consequences, or, if you know you'll be leaving for good and you want to deed your home to someone else, you can do that, too. You can even take your children with you—you just have to pay for their passports and visas. Homeownership, parenthood—the terms now resemble what they mean elsewhere in the world.

Sandra is doing more than talking about it. She's bought a house. Revision: Her Colombian husband bought her a house. And it's not quite a house, it's two rooms, a front room that's painted the dark pink of old roses in their last bloom, with a couch that spits me to the floor when I sit on it because the cushion isn't connected to the bench. After I've tried her number (disconnected) and her aunt's (no Jaqueline there, but the man who answered had heard of a woman named La China and would try to get her the message), Sandra called the number I'd left her (Alejandra's) and gave an address ten blocks from her old place. She's across the street from an empty factory, down another alleyway. I knocked on the door and Mia, who is now nearly four, answered.

Across from where I am splayed on the ground there is an overturned chair and a nightstand, made of black glossy wood, with children's shoes spilling out of its bottom half. Mia begins to pull shoes out of the pile. I sit on the ground and she shows me her favorite pairs: the clear jellies, the wood platforms with white pleather straps, and cute bright blue T-straps, but her favorites are the ones with pink marabou, which she doesn't know look like a Barbie version of what Marilyn Monroe might have worn. I stand up finally, brush myself off, put the cushion back on the sofa, and sit gingerly on it.

Sandra has not yet emerged from the back room, so I sit with Mia and let her model shoes for me. She has enormous dark eyes and waist-length black hair hoisted into a fuzzy side ponytail. Some of the sandals are broken, she points out; others are too big for her, she says, hand-me-downs from a neighbor. Sandra appears at the refrigerator in the back room, drinking a glass of water, pushing the hair out of her face and tipping her head back to drink. The front room is a living room and the back room holds a kitchenette, a bed, and a crib. She turns to me with the same "Hooooolia!" as ever. She is wearing black spandex shorts and a yellow lace-trimmed camisole. The shadows of her wide, dark nipples spread across the front. She looks the same, only older: same mole on the right side of her cheek, same big smile, more wrinkles, same darting black eyes.

All of her electric devices have failed her in the last week. Her cell phone, her blender: They are both broken and she will need new ones. Plus now she has no money. Her husband lives in Cali but comes to Havana every twenty days to spend ten days here with her and Mia and their ten-month-old daughter. He leaves Sandra with $500 each month, which supports her, but this past trip was cancelled for some reason or another and he didn't bring her money and she had to go down to the fountain at Paseo and *malecón* to try to earn some. They were married three years ago. It's their third anniversary around now, she says, and I press her to be more precise, because the math isn't adding up. The last time I saw her was two years ago on the *malecón* and she was with another man: short and skinny, making lively hand motions when he spoke. She had called him her boyfriend but he wasn't the

Colombian. She shakes her head and says she doesn't know what I'm talking about, she doesn't know who I'm describing because she's been married to Ivan for three years now and she never had any boyfriend like the one I'm describing.

"Mami!" Mia shouts. We turn to her. She wants to go to the fair down the street, a collection of mini-carousels and games that squat in a park where there used to be grass. She stands with her tiny hand on her tiny cocked-out hip and requests 5 pesos for the carnival ride, a two-story metal contraption that puts kids in a cage and swings them up and down in half-circles. Sandra asks if I have any Cuban pesos and I hand Mia a green five-peso bill. Mia looks at Sandra with narrowed eyes as Sandra says, "Don't ask any men for money this time, yahear?" and then, to me, "I've gotten complaints from neighbors about how she asks people for money for the rides."

Sandra doesn't wear a ring; she has nothing on her fingers today. She's not moving to Colombia, she says, because she wouldn't leave until she'd bought a place.

"What if he leaves me? What am I left with? Stranded in Cali with two babies, have to come back to Cuba to live with Aboo"—Aboo rents her own place down the alley from Sandra. "I'd have nothing," Sandra says. Now she has her two rooms in San Miguel, which are hers, really hers, signed over to her, and now she can go to Cali because as long as she returns for a visit every two years, they will stay hers. She just has to finish fixing up the bathroom first—she's only bought half the tiles she'll need but they cover the important part, the shower part.

There are no new restaurants or shops amid the defunct factories and de facto living spaces of San Miguel, and it takes just as long for a car to get down the pitted streets as it did two years ago. No one seems to be overseeing the carnival games, and as I get into the car that will take me back down-town, the gypsy cab driver who's waited for me all after-noon hopes aloud that the rusting metal leaves no children mangled or hurt. He's walked around it a few times and it seems unsafe. He lives in Vedado and once he'd taken me out here, he insisted on waiting. This neighborhood has gotten rougher, he says, and he won't charge for the ride back into town; he's heading back anyway and he feels better knowing he hasn't left me in a troublesome situation out here. The cops rarely come this deep into San Miguel anymore, he says. We drive away and I try to spot Mia in the crowd and think I see her white crop-top and black ponytail.

Consumers no longer need permits to buy renovation materials. In fact, the new laws for homeownership encour-age them to build. The banks are giving out small loans for exactly this purpose, though the complaint now is that there's not enough material to go around. This means that Katherine's house renovation has sped along. There's an airy new kitchen and a new studio in the back. Isnael is in the garage when I arrive, cutting wood for a canvas frame, and as I walk past, he calls my name. He's wearing clothes that were once white and are now covered in grime and swipes of blue, pink, green, yel-low, and black paint; but his clothes have the intention of white-ness, the clothing of recent Santería initiates in their year of dressing purely. He made saint last October. He wears all white and the bracelet of the initiated children of Yemayá. He's good, he says. Still working at Katherine's place, especially now that her husband's art is selling well. Isnael acts, nowadays, more like an artist's assistant, like a right-hand man, and he likes it. His work is here, now, and it's a good thing, he says. His faith is his faith and his work is his work.

The entrepreneurial sector of Cuba had hovered around 150,000 permits—for restaurants, rooms, other small businesses of which there were few until the range of options widened—until these current reforms. As of June 2012, there were 371,200 small businesses in Cuba. Money is floating around in the open now, trading hands from artist to assistant, from patron to chef and chef to waiter.

There are businesses everywhere. On one Old Havana street, in the unrenovated back area, there are two carpentry garages with crib sides and dressers and planks in progress. In a car repair garage, an old Ford hunkers up on stilts. A man at a cart peddles produce and it's avocado season, so he's propped the avocados on their round bases with their eyes pointing toward the sky. A street-front shop sells Chinese water filters and sticky lipstick, a pastry cart offers *señoritas* and *pasteles de guayaba* that put Sylvain's anemic sweets to shame.

Just down the street and to the left, toward the ocean, there are four people staffing a religious-objects store. In a country where religion used to be illegal, it's the busiest locale on the block. A sign in the front reads, "LA ENVIDIA ES LA RELIGION DE LOS MEDIOCRES"—envy is the religion of the mediocre—and the shop is thick with beaded necklaces in every imaginable color, and bracelets, urns, statuettes, wood bowls, sculptures, and maracas with shells on nets around them. The shelving extends twenty meters into the back of the house and six customers wait at two different counters. Down the street, Oasis Nelva sells potted succulents and palms and bonsai, which are advertised on professional-looking plastic in the windows. A man flattens out bumpy pots at a tinware shop across the street. Everywhere there is sound: grinding, sanding, the radio, a hammer, shouting.

I go to a "sport bar" called La Chucheria where I wait for a table behind two middle-aged women poring over the schedule for 3-D Extreme movie theater. Tickets cost $3. They sit down and a woman and teenage boy emerge, both dressed in a style I associate with any cosmopolitan world city—she in a shiny black asymmetrical raincoat and tight blue cotton skirt, he with big headphones around his neck—and she is distinctly Cuban as she chastises him for standing in the drizzle with their takeout, three pizzas and three milkshakes. She taps on a white iPhone and then tells someone she'll be a little late getting home; they're waiting out the rain. The waitresses wear matching black Nike tennis skirts and the customers sit in translucent plastic Philippe Starck chairs with the café name engraved on the back. Cuban reggaeton and Enrique Iglesias play low on a flat-screen above the porch. There is no toilet paper in the bathroom.

The people who are at these bars are the people who didn't used to go out. I go to another restaurant, a rooftop at which the women have silky dark hair and wear short satin shift dresses with pearls; the men are in polo shirts. These were the people who used to go to each others' houses only, parties at which Havana felt like a cinematic, glittery version of itself: beautiful women whirling, straight-shouldered men pouring drinks of white rum into plastic cups, mojitos until the mint ran out and then Cuba libres after, windows open in the winter or air conditioners in the living room in the summer. Now the glitter is on display in public; private businesses hand out printed receipts for the first time in my memory.

In these places, Havana is growing, creating room for ever more restaurant owners and shop owners to join the artists and the musicians in the conspicuous consumption in which we, the rest of the capitalist world, indulge. In these places, Havana could be anywhere else: Miami or Mexico City or the poshest restaurant in San Salvador. You could hop from lovely new bar to lovely new bar, surrounded by clusters of young locals for an entire trip. Two architects I know take me to a new bar down in Habana Vieja for drinks after their office closes on Friday afternoon and tell me that they're financially solvent for the first time in a long while. They show me a book with a private project they're working on. Quietly, of course, and in addition to what they're doing at their government day jobs, but they're doing something. I have to see this other bar, they say, and we go to another spot.

I used to go to spinning classes in the back room of the apartment of a woman named Iris, where, on the back porch, women drank water after class and traded the numbers of informal masseuses. Now the spinning is legal, the masseuses are legal, the carpentry business that Carlos's friend's stepfather had is legal. The architecture is illegal, still, but they're doing it anyway; businesspeople hoping to open restaurants with the backing of family abroad are trading the phone numbers of informal architects who will go to legal printing businesses and whip up very professional-looking packets and presentations of what they'll do to make the café as sophisticated as any in Mexico City.

The sense of precariousness remains. These businesses could be snatched away; someone with too many ties to the United States could be thrown in jail the way two foreign businessmen who were locked away for a year were; someone who is too critical, as dissident Oswaldo Payá was, could die under suspicious circumstances as he did last year. No one doubts who is still in power. So for some, these changes aren't anywhere near enough. Upon Lucía's first visit to Havana after leaving, she tells me that she won't go back until the Castros no longer occupy the helm of her country. It's just too sad. "It's strange," she tells me, "when you're in Cuba, you have no perspective on how bad things are, because you've never been anywhere else. And then you go somewhere else, and you return, and it's a different place."

Adela leaves for Ecuador in September. A visit, not a definitive exit. The *escuelas al campo*, where students like Isnael worked in the fields in a yearly solidarity exercise and which Adela got out of attending, have now been officially shuttered. Adrián is still in Europe.

/// This book is, in a way, the story of an exodus. Even if this generation has not physically left the island in its entirety, this generation has detached from its country's fate in some deep and meaningful way. Their impatient hopes and dreams are often disconnected from reality because in a circumscribed world, all change is fantastical. Distracted by the dominant uncertainty of their young adulthoods, they make few plans but the plans to leave. Perhaps the most apt factual representation is that they are not having children: In the seventies, there were ten babies born in Cuba for every Cuban who left, but in 2010, according to a national survey, that number had declined to three. Young people cite socioeconomic reasons and "family and personal reasons" for having fewer children than they'd like. Havana continues to hemorrhage its young and ambitious, graying ever faster.

Cuba is the country that stood up against the giant and continues to do so. Cuba is defined by what it is against: It is not connected to the rest of the capitalist world; it is against the United States and its cynical marketplace, its foreign involvement. It's a system built around politics and ideology and the security of those politics and that ideology, rather than built around and for the people who compose it. This generation is the first generation of Cubans among whom there is a consensus that discourse floats high above reality, is entirely untethered to what they're living. They are the last generation raised under Fidel, the first generation raised in globalization, the first generation to come into adulthood in a time when it's largely acknowledged that nothing works and they won't have an impact.

And yet this is not the story of an exodus, because there have been changes. Each five-year plan shifts things in Havana toward the rest of the world. Ten years ago, my college classmates and I invited the Cubans we met to make-shift parties on our dorm's front porch because they weren't allowed inside. Those parties had been covertly shut down by state security agents on our corner who quietly told the Cubans in attendance that they were violating the spirit if not the letter of the law. Guests whispered thank yous and left the party. Five years ago I could invite any Cuban anywhere. And five more years on, the lives of the people in this book have shifted: whether they made plans or pursued dreams or not, they are, for the most part, more rooted, in Cuba or elsewhere, in the way that lives inevitably change between twenty and twenty-five, twenty-five and thirty.

There's an air of futility to projecting into Cuba's future. At nearly every juncture, Fidel has done something unpredictable, something brilliant, made some last-ditch effort to maintain control and succeeded. Anywhere else, an increasingly wide divide between the rich and poor would generate tension; wealth and the ability to generate it creates empowerment and demands, and as the ration book is decreased, and as the old guard Communists die and the people who have only ever known not to count on the government for much more than fever medicine and seven pounds of rice per month grow up, the Castro regime must end. Raúl has said that he will step down when his second term ends, in 2018. And still, what would replace him is unclear. After nearly sixty years, who would take the place of a Castro? The strong alternatives left or died, were pushed out by the regime or gave in and started over elsewhere. If everyone who'd left in the last twenty years, in the last decade, even, would return, that's when things would change, an artist acquaintance tells me that August. So for the time being, since he's only thirty and 2018 isn't so far off, he'll stay.

There is some Sunday in every Wednesday in Havana, and there's also a blending of tomorrow and yesterday in today. Havana is a place where everyday existence is so rooted in the present moment, yet thought exists primarily in past or future tenses. Paradise is Cuba's goal and its context: What the island could be *if only*; what it once was. But there is no other side of paradise, no way to live in the nostalgic gloss of the past or to start construction of a life on the other side of the limitations of today. Predicting what will happen in Cuba in the next decade is an exercise in humility, because I assume that words on paper will be proven wrong. And so the revision, the recursive exercise that is involvement in Cuba, continues.

/// "The thing I have to remember that's just so strange," said Elaine, "is that when we park the car, I have to get out and look around and really remember exactly where I leave the car. Everything is so big, and everyone has new cars and they all look exactly the same."

This was among the first observations she made on my first visit to Miami, back in 2011, spoken while I was driving her to work at a kindergarten in southern Miami where she spent seven hours a day with Spanish-speaking toddlers.

I'd taken Nicolas to his boss's house earlier that morning so I could have the car while they worked. As we drove, Nicolas told me that he used to put the lunch Elaine made him every day in the trunk, to keep all of the seats in the car free. In Cuba, you never knew which acquaintance you'd give a ride to along the way, or who'd offer you $10 to go just a block or two farther than you were going anyway. In the United States, he'd said, everyone had papers and crap all over their back seats. Everyone drove alone. That weekend, when we went to Miami Beach to walk around and cheered at a Marlins game, Nicolas made me drive: He'd been chauffeur since they arrived, since Elaine hadn't yet taken the test, and he wanted a few days off.

Elaine and Nicolas had spent nearly all of the $4,500 they'd managed to save over their last few years in Havana on this car. Nicolas worked for a man who installed glass staircases in the homes of Miami's wealthy and ostentatious and followed up his twelve-hour days with certification classes to become an Electrician. Elaine had rotated through four low-paying child-care jobs since she'd arrived, because it was employment she could get without speaking English. But they were saving money in fits and starts: They lived with Nicolas's sister and her husband, who took good care of them. Nicolas still didn't have a cell phone.

Carlos's best friend, Ivan, had been in Miami for the first few months after Elaine and Nicolas's arrival but had to return to Cuba. He'd gotten a speeding ticket that he couldn't pay and didn't contest, so his license was revoked. When he kept driving anyway and got pulled over again, he'd been given a court date that he ignored. After a few months, he had wound up with a $4,000 fine and no money, so his mother, among Elaine's closest friends, bought him a plane ticket back home. If he ever wanted to live in the United States again, he'd have to pay the fine.

This sort of thing is part of what Nicolas loves about the United States: that there are consequences for actions that grow, step by step, rather than the specter of utter disaster that regulates actions in Havana. Nicolas has not looked back since he left. Nicolas is more American, I sometimes think, than I am: solid and hardworking and independent and real-istic, a nose-to-the-grindstone sort of man reinforcing the values of the country to which he's arrived.

That Ivan had left wouldn't be important until Carlos would visit Miami from where he was studying in Brazil and decide that he wanted to stay. By then, Elaine and Nico-las had different jobs cleaning medical facilities and Maykel, their younger son, had arrived, too. They had an apartment of their own and two cars. She didn't like Miami, Elaine said—reflexively conservative, with little of the intellec-tual life that had sustained her in Havana accessible to her, because people were spread too far apart for the casual visits of Havana and cultural activities were too expensive—but she said she couldn't imagine returning to Cuba, its insecu-rity, its black-market machinations, its ever-present politics, after living on the outside.

The next time I visit Miami, Elaine and Nicolas and Car-los and his brother have moved into a three-bedroom town-house in a gated Kendall community where swans and ducks roam the grounds. Carlos sleeps on the floor of his brother's room and my boyfriend and I have his room. It is Carlos's birthday and a group of twenty or so have gathered on their patio. One of the women who'd studied for the ISA test with him all those years ago arrived in Miami a month ago and she and her boyfriend are there, as well as Elaine's cousin and her husband, a handful of other acquaintances. Cuba rose like a balloon over all of us, shading every topic brought up as we talked about Havana. There seems to be no "never" when it comes to Cubans and Cuba. Elaine has a new plan now. With the new regulations, since Carlos is technically among the people who can legally spend two years outside the coun-try, she wants to try to keep her apartment, though no one else has remained in the building. The architect's daughter

upstairs has dumped the philandering art dealer and is applying for visas and even the apartment that Che personally
handed over is in the final phases of sale. Even after two years
in Miami and even with all of its flaws, I think Elaine would
rather live in Havana, and I think she hates that fact because
it defies her formidable intellect. What she tells me is, "I'm
an immigrant in this country. If I lose the apartment, my
home, then I lose it, but as long as I can I'll keep it. If there's a
change and things start to flow differently in Cuba, of course
I'll live there. Because now I'm free. Even if I went back, I
wouldn't be living there like in jail."

But for now—never mind next year in Havana, right now
in Miami—the *trovador* Descemer Bueno is doing a concert at
the new Friday night party that one of *los adolescentes*, who's
come up to Miami on a family visa, began. She used to be a
tall, genuine, sweet hippie girl, and now she's a tall beauty
in platform heels and an asymmetrical haircut who runs a
weekly fiesta called Vedado Social Club. I'm at the Vedado
Social Club party on the outdoor back patio of a bar in Wyn-
wood. Twinkling paper globe lanterns cast light from the
palm trees and I hear no English spoken. Descemer Bueno
is playing songs I've heard so many times before, and after
every six people who pass where Carlos and I stand, I turn to
him and say, "Do I know him?" To which he responds, "Yes,
you could recognize him, he's from Havana, he's friends with
so-and-so," and we do this so many times that it makes me a
little dizzy. By the time the night is winding down and we are
standing at the door, getting ready to go, someone taps the
mic and says, *damas y caballeros*, Carlos Varela.

And I'm twenty again, sitting at the Plaza Vieja a decade
ago after a night at the *morro* club, four or so in the morning and no one else is at the plaza except a lone waiter in a
bow tie and waistcoat and the buildings laugh shadows and

yellow moldings in the light of the sepia streetlamps. I've just arrived to study for the semester and am with a Cuban acquaintance. We've been dancing all night and I don't know where I am exactly, or what time it is, just that the sky will be bright again in an hour or two. I'm sitting in a cast-iron chair drinking a rum and TuKola and the only Cuban singer whose music I know, Carlos Varela, is here; he must be a friend of a friend. Someone puts a guitar in his arms, and he plays the guitar for a few songs' worth of time. They're songs about love and patriotism and family and the music bounces across the plaza. It's a moonlit moment that, even as it unfolds, I know I will remember. And I do; it's the moment that catches in my mind when someone mentions Havana for the decade that follows, one of the memories that I pull out and examine from different angles when I live in Havana and the city feels too hot, sad, anxious. Havana is also that moment, I will remind myself, it's the sadness and the magic and the luck, losing the passport and finding it.

Carlos Varela is playing a concert here next weekend, the posters say. He is right off the plane from Havana, probably taking a week in Florida to visit friends and family, shop before his show. He's done a few concerts in Miami recently; U.S. visas have been more easily granted to Cuban professionals lately. I imagine that if I was closer to the stage I could smell Cuban laundry detergent. The coincidence feels amazing, that I am here for one weekend and he is playing just one song. Carlos and I listen near the back, our arms around one another, and I think: Havana is this moment, too, and the loop that connects the two.

ACKNOWLEDGMENTS

I owe this book to those who generously lent me access to their lives and thoughts: Lucía, the Reyes family, Liván, Sandra, Isnael, Adrián, and Adela before anyone else. I am endlessly grateful to them and to the people around them who opened their doors to me, included me in gatherings and discussions, and answered my questions, whether interesting, or vaguely rude or obvious, or all of the above. I hope I have done well by the trust they placed in me.

Thank you to the Havana family, the village—Matthew and Jana, Pamela, Raul, and Aimara for conversation, insight, and odd and necessary kindnesses—and to Alejandro, Nicole, Claire, Aviva, Tricina, Tara, Megan, and the women of Writing Corps for reading, inspiring, and listening at phases early and late. I admire and owe Elaine and Carlos much more than I can fully express here. Endless thanks to Patrick for the IV line of support, intellect, and optimism that he's offered throughout.

Various professors and writers affiliated with Columbia University were instrumental in helping me hone the ideas and the rhetoric of this book: Richard Locke, Lis Harris, Patricia O'Toole, Mark Lamster, Rivka Galchen, Stephen O'Connor, and Phillip Lopate. Thank you. Enormous thanks to my agent, Diana Finch, who stuck with this book from its raw beginning; my editor, Laura Mazer, who stewarded it into existence with sensitivity, honesty, and enthusiasm; and to the Norman Mailer Center and my fellow fellows there.

Mine may be, I think, among the very few families that not only refrains from strangulation on family trips but is actually often at our best while navigating someplace new together. For this and so much else, I am grateful to my mother, father, and sister.

SELECTED BIBLIOGRAPHY

In addition to many news articles—primarily those written by the heroically thorough Havana-based staff of Reuters, but also published by *The New York Times*, the BBC, and the *Wall Street Journal*—the following books and magazine articles were instrumental for the research of this book.

Arenas, Reinaldo. *Before Night Falls*. New York: Penguin, 1994.

Bangs, Lester. *Main Lines, Blood Feasts, and Bad Taste: A Lester Bangs Reader*. New York: Random House, 2008.

Bardach, Ann Louise. *Cuba Confidential: Love and Vengeance in Miami and Havana*. New York: Random House, 2007.

Benjamin, Walter W. *Selected Writings: 1913–1926*. Cambridge: Harvard University Press, 1996.

Bishop, Claire. "Speech Disorder: On Tania Bruguera at the 10th Havana Biennial." *Artforum* 47, no. 10 (June 2009): 121–122.

Block, Holly, and Gerardo Mosquera. *Art Cuba: The New Generation*. New York: Harry N. Abrams, 2001.

Cabezas, Amalia L. *Economies of Desire: Sex and Tourism in Cuba and the Dominican Republic*. Philadelphia: Temple University Press, 2009.

Chomsky, Aviva, Barry Carr, and Pamela Maria Smorkaloff. *The Cuba Reader: History, Culture, Politics*. Durham, NC: Duke University Press, 2009.

Corrales, Javier, and Mario Pecheny. *The Politics of Sexuality in Latin America: A Reader on Lesbian, Gay, Bisexual, and Transgender Rights*. Pittsburgh: University of Pittsburgh Press, 2010.

Didion, Joan. *Miami*. 1st Vintage International ed. New York: Vintage, 1998.

Eaton, Tracey. "Beyond Fake Boogie Boards: Promoting Democracy in Cuba." The Pulitzer Center for Crisis Reporting. June 4, 2011. http://pulitzercenter.org/articles/pro-democracy-cuba-beyond-fake-boogie-boards.

Estrada, Alfredo José. *Havana: Autobiography of a City*. New York: Palgrave Macmillan, 2008.

Farber, Samuel. *Cuba Since the Revolution of 1959: A Critical Assessment*. Chicago: Haymarket Books, 2011.

Gómez, José Miguel Sánchez. "We're Bad Cuz Nobody Loves Us, Nobody Loves Us Cuz We're Bad." *In These Times*, December 2009.

Gutierrez, Pedro Juan. *Dirty Havana Trilogy: A Novel in Stories*. New York: HarperCollins, 2002.

Hamilton, Carrie, and Elizabeth Dore. *Sexual Revolutions in Cuba: Passion, Politics, and Memory*. Chapel Hill, NC: University of North Carolina Press, 2012.

Infante, Guillermo Cabrera. *Mea Cuba*. New York: Farrar, Strauss and Giroux, 2994.

Lewis, Michael. "Commie Ball: A Journey to the End of a Revolution." *Vanity Fair*, July 1, 2008. http://www.vanityfair.com/politics/features/2008/07/cuban_baseball200807.

Marx, Gary. "False Pretenses." *Chicago Tribune*, April 27, 2003.

Moore, Robin. *Music and Revolution: Cultural Change in Socialist Cuba*. Berkeley: University of California Press, 2006.

Morales Domínguez, Esteban. *The Challenges of the Racial Problem in Cuba*. Havana: Fundación Fernando Ortiz, 2007.

Ojito, Mirta A. *Finding Mañana: A Memoir of a Cuban Exodus*. New York: Penguin, 2005.

Pearlman, Ellen. "The Fallacy of Utopia: The Art World and Current Dialectic in Havana, Cuba." *Brooklyn Rail*, July 1, summer 2002. http://www.brooklynrail.org/2002/07/art/the-fallacy-of-utopia-the-artworld-and-current-dialectic-in-havana-cuba.

Pérez Sarduy, Pedro. *Afro-Cuban Voices: On Race and Identity in Contemporary Cuba*. Gainesville: University Press of Florida, 2000.

Peters, Philip. "Cuba's Entrepreneurs: Foundation of a New Private Sector." The Lexington Institute, Arlington, July 31, 2012.

Smith, Lois M., and Alfred Padula. *Sex and Revolution: Women in Socialist Cuba*. New York: Oxford University Press, 1996.

Stock, Ann Marie. *Framing Latin American Cinema: Contemporary Critical Perspectives*. Minneapolis: University of Minnesota Press, 1997.

Symmes, Patrick. *The Boys from Dolores: Fidel Castro's Schoolmates from Revolution to Exile*. New York: Random House, 2008.

Thomas, Hugh. *Cuba, or, the Pursuit of Freedom*. Updated ed. New York: Da Capo Press, 1998.

ABOUT THE AUTHOR

Journalist Julia Cooke's writing has appeared in *Condé Nast's Traveller, The Atlantic, Guernica, LA Weekly, The Wall Street Journal, The Virginia Quarterly Review, Gawker, The Village Voice, The Christian Science Monitor,* and many other publications. She has been a Nonfiction Fellow at the Norman Mailer Writers Colony and a Hertog Fellow at Columbia University, where she earned her MFA. She lives in New York City and teaches at the New School. *The Other Side of Paradise* is her first book.

Fast Tim... .... *...meland*, by
Par... ...y moving
acc.. ...daily events
that a.. s, ...d weddings)
as well as ...violence, trauma, and political divisions that are particular to
the country.

Es Cuba: Life and Love on an Illegal Island, by Lea Aschkenas. $15.95,
978-1-58005-179-8. This triumphant love story captures a beautiful and
intangible sense of sadness and admiration for the country of Cuba and for
its people.

Breathless: An American Girl in Paris, by Nancy K. Miller. $16.00, 978-1-
58005-488-1. This provocative coming-of-age memoir is set in sultry 1960s
Paris, offering a glimpse into the intimate lives of girls before feminism.

Tango: An Argentine Love Story, by Camille Cusumano. $15.95, 978-1-
58005-250-4. The spicy travel memoir of a woman who left behind a failed
fifteen-year relationship and fell in love with Argentina through the dance
that embodies intensity, freedom, and passion.

*A Thousand Sisters: My Journey into the Worst Place on Earth to Be
a Woman,* by Lisa Shannon, foreword by Zainab Salbi. $16.95, 978-1-58005-
359-4. Through her inspiring story of turning what started as a solo 30-mile
run to raise money for Congolese women into a national organization, Run for
Congo Women, Lisa Shannon sounds a deeply moving call to action for each
person to find in them the thing that brings meaning to a wounded world.

Wanderlust: A Love Affair with Five Continents, by Elisabeth Eaves.
$16.95, 978-1-58005-311-2. A love letter from the author to the places she's
visited—and to the spirit of travel itself—that documents her insatiable
hunger for the rush of the unfamiliar and the experience of encountering new
people and cultures.

Find Seal Press Online
www.SealPress.com
www.Facebook.com/SealPress
Twitter: @SealPress